THIS PLAY IS DEDICATED to the late Fr. Dunstan Jones, OFM Cap., and the Capuchin Franciscans for their great work and love for the people of Papua New Guinea. Fr. Dunstan shared the Huli folktale of SumiSami to Ray and son Larkin when they visited him in Papua New Guinea in 2002. He was the first waitman (whiteman) to witness the story and stunning beauty of SumiSami.

SumiSami was first published in the United States as a paperback original by Lambing Press, PO BOX 23262, Pittsburgh PA 15222.

SumiSami (c) 2021 Ray Werner

Ray Werner has asserted his right to be identified as the writer of this work.

ISBN 978-1-950607-02-0

BOOK DESIGN: Larkin Werner

PHOTO CREDITS: cover, page vii, J.L. Martello/18ricco; page 122, Annie O'Neill

PRINTED in the USA

CAUTION: All rights whatsoever in this pla y are strictly reserved. Requests to reproduce the text in whole or in part should be addressed to the publisher.

AMATEUR AND PROFESSIONAL PERFORMING RIGHTS. No performance of any kind may be given unless a license has been obtained. Applications should be made before rehearsals begin. Publication of this play does not necessarily indicate its availability for performance.

APPLICATIONS FOR PERFORMANCE should be emailed to: ray_werner@yahoo.com

SumiSami and all its characters are entirely from the writer's imagination. Any resemblance to real persons living or deceased is strictly coincidental.

COVER: The Franciscan tau is the last letter of the early Hebrew alphabet (tav), which for Christians represents the end of the Old Testament, and the beginning of the New. Also in the shape of a cross, St. Francis adopted it as the symbol of his new community of friars. It's superimposed over the character Moses, played by actor Wali Jamal.

March 1, 2022

For Chuck,

Thanks for all you've done for so many & for your friendship over the years

Ray

SumiSami

A TRAGEDY IN THREE ACTS.

RAY WERNER

The Commitment of the Capuchins

PAPUA NEW GUINEA remains perhaps the most primitive country in the world. Still, the Capuchin Franciscan Friars are committed to bringing the Catholic faith, education and a better way of life to these beautiful, struggling people.

That commitment took root in 1955, when six young Capuchins arrived at Tari in the Southern Highlands, the setting for SumiSami. Fr. Dunstan Jones, OFM Cap, to whom this play is dedicated, arrived in 1962.

Today, PNG still must endure corrupt governments and the greed of foreign interests plundering their vast resources. But the Capuchin Franciscans, in the spirit of our founder St. Francis, are determined. And stories inspired by our heroic Brothers help us endure.

It was an honor for Brother Ray Ronan and I to advise the playwright and help enrich SumiSami with the colorful Tok Pisin (pidgin) language and Huli culture.

Lukim yu long now.

Bishop Bill Fey, OFM Cap.

SUMISAMI

SumiSami premiered at The Ray Werner Play Festival on November 8 through December 2, 2018 at Pittsburgh Playwrights Theatre in Pittsburgh's Cultural District, with the following cast and crew.

Mark Clayton Southers *Producing Artistic Director*
Monteze Freeland *Play Festival Artistic Director*
John Amplas *Director*

PATA PADDY David Cabot*
CLARE Nami Talbot
MOSES Wali Jamal
ALOIS Devon Burton
PATA TOM Gabe DeRose

Hope Marie *Stage Manager*
Diane Melchitzky *Design/Construction*
Mark Whitehead *Sound Design*
Piper Clement *Lighting Design*
Cheryl El-Walker *Costume and Makeup Design*
Arionna Sherwood *Props Master*
Austin Sills *Lighting*
Ashley Southers *Lighting Tech*
James Howard, Eric Eleam, Jr. *Crew*
Michelle Belan *Marketing*

* Actor appears courtesy of Actors' Equity

SUMISAMI

SumiSami
A TRAGEDY IN THREE ACTS.

Characters

PATA PADDY, OFM Cap., *missionary* 40's

CLARE, *lovely Huli girl* 18

MOSES, *a Huli elder* 50's

ALOIS, *Huli boy* 18

PATA TOM, OFM Cap., *missionary* 20's

Act One
September, 1975, the Capuchin mission of Tari, evening and late evening.

Act Two
The next morning, afternoon and early evening.

Act Three
The next day, the day of independence.
And late morning, a week following.

TIME:

Four days in September, 1975. Two days before and the Day of Independence for Papua New Guinea, and the morning a week following.

PLACE:

The village and Capuchin mission outpost of Tari, in the remote Southern Highlands of Papua New Guinea.

SETTING:

The mission, the jungle, the rainforest, and the mountainous Southern Highlands of Papua New Guinea. The scenes are a mountain trail, the exterior of the mission, the top of the SumiSami cliff, the interior of a thatched hut which serves as an office, classroom, kitchen, bedroom and mission of the two Capuchins. We can go from the jungle to the interior of the mission or wherever we want as the lighting, a few props and sound design direct us. The flow of SumiSami is like a river which is calm at its source and turbulent as it falls quickly over large boulders and calm again as it levels in the valley below. We are in a dugout canoe on this river, never knowing when we will hit the rapids, but we know they are there.

PRODUCTION NOTES:

The Huli is a tribe of red-black skinned Papuans who have been living in the Southern Highlands of PNG for countless generations. The folktale of SumiSami (SUmeeSAHmi) is one of their legends.

WARDROBE:

Paddy and Tom wear the traditional Capuchin brown habit, with the cord and the cowl, the tau (the Capuchin wooden cross), sandals, and when not in their habit, they wear hiking boots, shirt, shorts. Paddy has a long, full, but rather scraggly beard and doesn't care much about his appearance. And a very colorful hat, his trademark. Tom has a neatly trimmed beard, and is conscious about his appearance. Alois and Clare wear bright, colorful "seconhan clos," with a preference for red, and no shoes. Moses also wears colorful seconhan clos, including a lap lap, a sort of skirt. Around his neck he has a necklace of small bones.

SOUND DESIGN:

Throughout, drums, including the wooden drum of PNG, punctuate the action, evoke different moods — love and tenderness, mystery, foreboding terror. Flute and guitar embellish the sound. Over the multi-image, it is primitive, evocative.

VIDEO AND MULTI-IMAGE:

As we are coming into the theater, images of the wigmen and mudpeople of PNG, early photos of the first bush planes, first Capuchins, the faces of natives, vibrant, raw, earthy, in black and white, in sync with the music — projected on the walls of the set, the theater, dissolving one to the other. Fade out before curtain rises. Later, these will come to life in living color.

LANGUAGE:

Pidgin (Tok Pisin) is interspersed throughout. It is a colorful and vibrant language cut out of the whole cloth of English, made up of English expressions. It is inventive and has a smile to it, and a captivating rhythm. It is used for texture, to draw us in and to heighten tension.

Note: A glossary of Tok Pisin words and expressions follows at the end of the play.

SUMISAMI

Act One
Scene One

Outside the mission, by a river, off.

AT RISE:

SFX: Drums, soft, mysterious.

ALOIS is sitting on his haunches near the river, which is just beyond him. He is in deep thought. He picks up a pebble and tosses it into the stream.

A thought strikes him, he takes out a small pad and writes something down.

ALOIS: My love has wings, my Clare… my love… yes… has wings…

SFX: Drums segue to a static radio, an announcer VO.

Lights down.

Act One
Scene Two

The mission, interior.

Pata Paddy O Hara is listening intently to the radio news, with considerable static. He has the volume turned up and his ear to it. The announcer has an Australian accent.

RADIO ANNOUNCER, VO: …but in the middle of all this, the day of independence still looms over the entire country as a day that will bring many changes to Papua New Guinea and many questions remain as to what the final outcome will be. Nevertheless, this already unruly capital city of Port Moresby has become a bit rowdy in recent days in anticipation of this enormous event just a few days from now…

VO continues under the first few lines of dialogue.

CLARE enters, carrying neatly folded clothes. She puts them on a side table, moves quietly about, picking up a few things, tidying up, shaking her head at the slight disarray. It's a bit like a bachelor's flat.

CLARE: *Picking up dirty clothes off the floor.* Ohhh... tsk... tsk... doti, doti... pata, doti clothes for bag, no floor. Plis.

PADDY: *Turning the volume up a little.* You are so right, Clare. Sorry.

RADIO ANNOUNCER, VO: ...but the preparations at the parliament building signal a once in a lifetime event for Papua New Guineans and it will be a celebration without precedent in its history as it prepares to govern itself for the very first time and the...

CLARE: Yes, I so right. What is Inglis word... dotipela?

PADDY: *Still glued to the radio.* Sloppy.

CLARE: Sluppy. Yu sluppy. My goodness... also... my gracious.

PADDY: Clare, please, I'm trying to listen...

RADIO ANNOUNCER, VO: ...orderly transition from Australian direct rule is expected to be historical in itself and they're hoping will set an example of how a democratic government that the Aussies have used with great effect...

CLARE: Dinner... do special kau kau... and someting from gaden ... you want now?

PADDY: No, we'll wait for Pata Tom. He should be back. Clare, don't you want to hear what's going on?

CLARE: *Ignores his question.* Waitim Pata Tom... ok...

RADIO ANNOUNCER, VO: ...over their great history will be a harbinger for the constitutional monarchy adopted by the new PNG government. Please stay tuned to this station...

SFX: Static increases.

PADDY: *Turing the radio off.* Darn radio… Not worth a lick…

CLARE: Ol taim waitem Pata Tom, olsem wonem?

PADDY: Please, Clare, speak English, not tok pisin, you must learn your English.

CLARE: Wait Pata Tom always why?

PADDY: He is still new. Sometimes he forgets. We must be patient.

CLARE: What is… patient? Sicman? Yes?

PADDY: Ha. Yes, sick man, but here, in this case, it means… to not get angry… to be calm… no belhat, Clare, no belhat.

CLARE: Laughs. Oh, understand. Plis. Tok pisin, Pata.

PADDY: Got me. One for you… Clare…

CLARE: Yes, Pata?

PADDY: Are you excited about the day after tomorrow?

CLARE: Day afta? Monday, Thursday… Wednesday, Sande, Fraide… day all same to Clare.

PADDY: Clare, the day after tomorrow, Papua New Guinea gains its freedom. Have you forgotten? Our day of independence. It is history. Just imagine!

CLARE: Hmm. Day In-de-pen-dunce. Clare no care so much. Wait see. Port Moresby big city. Many raskols big city. Clare laik Tari. Live here.

PADDY: Aren't people talking about it? Aren't they excited?

CLARE: They tok. Toktoktok.

PADDY: Well, I'm excited. And you should be, too. Papua New Guinea has a great future… Everyone will benefit… And, we'll get rid of those rascals in the big city.

The light begins to flicker. They both look at it and react.

CLARE: Ohhh… on off on off, pata….

PADDY: On off, yes… trouble somewhere…

CLARE: Trouble, all right, oh, my…

PADDY: The generator is on the bum…

CLARE: *Patting her behind.* On de bum… bum?

PADDY: Ha, forget the bum. The generator… is broken, that's the word. No wok. Bagarap.

CLARE: Yes, no wok… on de bum… *Pats her behind and laughs.* Inglis funny.

PADDY: Now, where did you learn that?

CLARE: From yu. Yu bin skulim mi, mi save. Yu tisim, I learn. Bum. *Pats her behind again.*

PADDY: Don't remember everything I teach you. Is Moses about? Moses mi stop we?

CLARE: Moses stop klostu. Moses fixim.

PADDY: He was able to fix it last time. Just when we had it going really good. Thought we solved that problem…

MOSES enters. Light continues to flutter.

MOSES: Pata, got planti problem.

PADDY: Don't make it too big, Moses. We need that generator.

MOSES: Raskols, pata. Stilim petrol.

PADDY: Not the rascals again. Have we some more petrol tucked away somewhere?

MOSES: Nogat, pata, raskols stilim all petrol, why I say planti problem.

Light continues to flicker, then dim, and slowly fade to black over the dialogue.

Lights up on PATA TOM, in the jungle. He is standing very still, looking at something. He is glued to it.

PADDY: Let's go figure this out, Moses. Back to the dark ages, as if we ever left it.

CLARE: Dark ages, Pata?

PADDY: It's history. Happened before. Taim bipo.

CLARE: Taim bipo, all right.

As they exit, the lights go all the way out.

MOSES: Damn raskols, no gut.

CLARE: No gut, all right.

PADDY: No need to swear. But you're right, damn raskols.

Act One
Scene Three

The jungle.

TOM stands motionless, looking at something. He's transfixed. He takes a few steps forward, not wanting to make a noise, or disturb what he sees. Whatever it is, he can't take his eyes off it.

SFX: *Drums punctuate the mystery.*

TOM cautiously takes a step forward.

SFX, OFF: *A woman's voice. High pitched, soft, sweet.* Ohhhaaaaeee.

TOM'S curiosity changes to mild shock.

SFX, OFF: *Again, the woman's voice.* Oheeeeeahhh…

TOM begins backing away, but still he watches, consumed by it.

Act one
Scene Four

The mission, interior. Later that evening.

Lights up on the humble Capuchin mission. There are a two oil lamps lit so the light is muted. PADDY paces back and forth, reverently reading from his breviary, almost out loud.

SFX: The drums. After a moment, a motorcycle approaches, pulls to a stop, outside.

PADDY pauses, turns towards the sound, goes back to his breviary.

TOM enters.

PADDY puts his breviary down, gives TOM a hearty welcome.

PADDY: Hey, Tom.

TOM: Paddy.

As they chat, TOM goes to the washstand and rinses his face, hands, dries off, retrieves his habit from a hook, puts it on over his clothes.

PADDY: Afraid you may have gotten eaten.

TOM: Made an offering of myself, but no takers.

PADDY: Good. We can use you around here.

TOM: Yeah… Oh, no, oil lamps, don't tell me, Paddy…

PADDY: Yes, the generator's not working…

TOM: Not again. Surely we don't have to order another part from Brisbane and wait six weeks in the dark.

PADDY: No. The rascals were at it again, this time stole our gasoline. Siphoned the tank and stole the reserves.

TOM: Paddy, we have to keep the gasoline under lock and key, at all times.

PADDY: Broke the lock, I'm afraid, the rascals.

TOM: Rascals. Makes them sound like cute little kids full of mischief.

PADDY: That's what I love about pidgin.

TOM: They're criminals.

PADDY: Rascals, criminals... pathetic thieves in any language. I'll try a bigger lock.

TOM: *Loses it for a moment.* No electricity. So no radio. No news tonight, the one thing I look forward to. No lights. No refrigeration. My reading. My god, these wretches. They'd steal your soul if they could sell it.

PADDY: Luckily, no buyer for souls, except the devil, and he strikes no bargain. And nothing in the fridge to spoil, nothing but water. Ha. Might still be a little cool, would you like some?

TOM: I would. Thank you. I'll get it.

PADDY: No bother.

PADDY gets the water for both of them, pours two glasses.

PADDY: How was your day?

TOM: That cycle isn't worth dog do. Rabbit do. Bird of Paradise do.

PADDY: We can do without the do, but not without the cycle.

TOM: Stalled on me going up that last steep hill into Pangia. Spent an hour cleaning the carburetor, messing with it...

PADDY: Nooo. Had it working fine yesterday, ran like a gem. So... how was your day?

TOM: What have we been talking about?

PADDY: The b-m-w. That's not your day. The first is a way of transportation. The second is a way of life. Ha.

TOM: Spare me, Pata.

CLARE enters with dinner, places it on the table, fusses about, ignoring their conversation. TOM notices her.

TOM: Sorry, Paddy. Not the best day. Hello Clare.

CLARE: Apinoon, Pata Tom.

TOM: *To PADDY.* There was a killing last night. A man was murdered with a machete, hacked to death — over a pig. From the Rewani family. I had his funeral mass before I left.

PADDY: Oh, my, that's terrible. How is his family doing?

TOM: Strange. Acted as though it was… expected. They were sad, of course. But more saddened by something else. He was hunting alone when he was killed. When they found him, his right thigh was missing… I learned a new word today. Kewa nui.

PADDY: Kewa nui, oh, no. Cannibalism. Unfortunate.

TOM: These people are crazy. Killing a man over a pig. And then eating his leg. Savages.

PADDY: A few still believe they receive their enemy's strength and courage if they eat some of their flesh.

TOM: The family was justified in being angry. I told them so.

PADDY: Alois, he saw this coming. Told me this could happen.

TOM: Alois? He saw it coming? I don't understand.

PADDY: The dispute was over the death of a daughter. And her bride wealth, her dowry. The dowry was a pig. Three years ago, I married this couple. Turned out to be a no good. Abusive. Had many women. After a year of this abuse, to get even with her husband, huh? she hung herself from the Wagie bridge… Her dangling feet barely touched the water. Payback. Moses found her, and cut her down. He was so angry.

TOM: What kind of payback is that, to take your own life? Absurd.

PADDY: Not uncommon with abused women in Papua New Guinea. The wife takes her own life, knowing that the payback will be… the husband's shame, and he will be held responsible for her death, and must also return the dowry, the pig. But… he can also pay with his life. Yes. Everyone understands this.

TOM: Payback, the social justice of savages. And they call themselves Christian. Catholic. Won't they at least try to find the murderer, bring him to justice?

PADDY: *Laughs at the absurdity of it.* It's payback, Tom. A debt is satisfied. The police will pretend to investigate, but want no part of it. Noooo. And life goes on.

TOM: An eye for an eye, savages.

PADDY: Clare, is dinner ready?

CLARE: You say wait Pata Tom, so Pata Tom come, so… *Places dishes on the table, serves dinner.* …Ok, kam na kisim.

PADDY: English, please, Clare.

CLARE: Ok, come and yu get it.

PADDY: This is why we have marriage instructions for young lovers, why we have to counsel married couples having problems. Essential.

TOM: What's the payback for all we do for them? Does it work both ways?

PADDY: It does. And our reward will be great. Have you forgotten?

CLARE puts finishing touches on the table.

TOM: Yes, you're right. As I said, just a bad day.

PADDY: Well, you must be hungry. Clare, you can cook sweet potatoes more cleverly than anyone.

CLARE: Welcom yu, Pata Paddy.

TOM: Might be a thousand ways to cook sweet potatoes, but there's only one way they taste. The same. God, what I'd give for a plate of mama's lasagne right now.

PADDY: Well, with a little imagination…

TOM: Paddy, must you always be the eternal optimist? Honestly.

They sit down at the table.

PADDY: Eternity. And optimism. Good idea for a sermon, Tom. Tenkyu tru.

CLARE: Ok, put dotipela dish… sink, ok?

As CLARE serves the greens, TOM takes an interest in her, watches CLARE intently as she finishes serving.

PADDY: We enjoy doing the dishes, Clare, you know that.

TOM: Clare, thank you for dinner.

CLARE: *Exiting, turns and smiles.* Welcom yu, Pata Tom.

TOM: What's this beside the sweet potato?

PADDY: Kumu, they call it. We call it greens. Clare boiled it with some herbs, looks like. Very tasty.

TOM: *Tasting it with his fingers.* And what does one use to keep it down?

PADDY: Ha. A Capuchin specialty. Obedience.

TOM: The Capuchins even have the food telling them what to do in Papua New Guinea.

TOM sticks a fork into a sweet potato, about to take a bite, when PADDY interrupts with the blessing. They make the sign of the cross.

PADDY: Father, we thank you for the goodness of your heart, to bless us with so much, for the richness of this life, to be able to help so many. Please strengthen us with every challenge of every day, the delight of every morning, the solitude of our brotherhood, and the comfort of your magnificence. Amen.

They bless themselves again at the end.

TOM: Very nice. Thank you, Paddy. And thank you for waiting dinner

PADDY: I thought there was enough gasoline in the jeep to make it to Mendi, so I sent Moses. Hope he makes it back before dark. I don't like these roads at night. We shouldn't be without our generator much longer.

TOM: Do you really trust Moses? How do you know it wasn't Moses who siphoned the gasoline?

PADDY: Tom, how could you? Can't you see the goodness in him?

TOM: Too trusting, Paddy. They get away with murder around you. Oh, sorry, poor choice of words.

PADDY: Moses has been my right hand forever. The Huli call him their sa-ve man, huh? Man i gut planti sa-ve. Said to have secret powers.

TOM: He's secretive, all right. Can't get through to him. He ignores me. Doesn't like me. Has very little to say around me. Don't know what it is.

PADDY: Patience. It requires great patience.

TOM: In short supply of that lately, I'm afraid.

PADDY: Moses is the keeper of the legends. He has taught Alois all he knows, and the more we know of the Huli, the more effective we will be. And what about Alois? How is it with you and Alois?

Lights up on ALOIS, still looking off, into the river. He has a certain stature, confidence.

TOM: All right, I suppose. Alois is a good boy. A boy? Nearly a man, I suspect.

PADDY: He is a man. And he is Huli. So when you're old enough to marry, you're a man. Alois. Ha. There's a poet in him.

ALOIS sits on his haunches studies what he's written.

TOM: He writes poetry? Is it any good?

PADDY: I've never seen it. Don't know if he actually writes any. Suspect he does.

TOM: Then how could you know if he's a poet? Honestly.

PADDY: I see poetry in the way he looks at life. Poetry in the way he talks about his love for Papua New Guinea. He has a great reverence for taim befo — the past. There's poetry in his heart. He was in my first catechist class, you know.

TOM: No, I didn't know that.

PADDY: Took to it right away. Excellent student. His English near perfect. And a good Huli, too, admires the culture, the history. I have learned a great deal from him.

TOM: I have yet to learn anything from these people, I'm afraid. Don't know how you do it.

Lights down on ALOIS.

PADDY: I love my people.

TOM: How long have you been here, Paddy. Ten years?

PADDY: Eleven years. Well, twelve, come next Spring. They've flown by, I can't believe it. Nearly one year for yourself, isn't it?

TOM: Eleven months and three days.

PADDY: You have an anniversary coming. We'll celebrate.

TOM: Celebrate? With what?

PADDY: Ha. Sweet potatoes, of course.

TOM: The longest year of my life. The days drag, even with so much to do, I don't know… I'm trying, Paddy, I am… And I don't want to complain, I really don't…

PADDY: Listen, you're doing great. Don't get discouraged. The motorcycle, the generator, the rascals, the food — I better not go on, huh? Ha. Those are just incidentals, a bit of grit on the landscape. Let it all... just happen to you. Why, just today, think about today, and what it meant to the Rewani family for you to be there for them.

TOM: But I didn't stay. I wanted to get back to... this.

PADDY: Yes. Home.

TOM: Home? Hardly that... home... Paddy, don't you miss anything, for the Lord's sake, anything at all?

PADDY: Of course, Tom. I miss... I miss my father whistling Paper Doll.

TOM: You miss... what?

PADDY: My father would go out onto the back porch of our little house... and whistle Paper Doll... and his favorite chickens would come squawking up to the back door for a little corn... every evening after dinner. Some evenings... I find myself whistling Paper Doll. My dad is dead these many years. But his Paper Doll and his chickens are still very much alive. And... I miss my mother singing love songs.

TOM: You're a sentimental fool, Paddy.

PADDY: She would be glad hear you say so. Everything reminded her of a song. If she heard you say sentimental fool, she'd start singing... *Sings.* "...gonna take, a sentimental journey, sentimental journey home..."

TOM: *Annoyed.* Paddy, give it a break...

PADDY: ...I believe you're a little homesick, Tom. Have to get your mind off it.

TOM: Perhaps you're right.

PADDY: Tom... Get any sense today of how the people are feeling about the day after tomorrow?

TOM: Thursday?

PADDY: The day of our independence. Now don't tell me you've forgotten…

TOM: Of course not. But I haven't thought much about it, either. So much happening, with the man killed, the funeral…

PADDY: They have no idea. We must help them see the significance.

TOM: These people never change. Day to day drudgery and they trust no one.

PADDY: They're right to be cautious. Everyone has taken advantage of them. The Dutch… Indonesians… the Australians… even some of the missionaries — stealing their gold, their copper, even their heritage. But our people have a great heart, a beautiful soul, and great curiosity.

TOM: They didn't boil him for supper?

PADDY: They would have roasted him… Ha… tastes much better.

TOM: Collecting recipes, Pata?

PADDY: I asked my first catechist class if anyone had ever eaten human flesh. A few hands went up. I asked, what did it taste like? They said… switmor… sweet. It tasted sweet.

TOM: And you think these people are ready for independence, to govern themselves?

PADDY: Absolutely. More than capable. All they need is the opportunity.

TOM: Don't forget motivation.

PADDY: Good, Tom, yes. Get excited about it. They have to see that in us. It will go a long way.

TOM: Paddy, what… what was the most difficult adjustment for you? …if it's not too personal…

PADDY: Oh, the heat, the heat, when I was in Port Moresby, couldn't stand it, thought I'd never make it, so coming here to the Highlands, a godsend.

TOM: *Laughs.* A godsend, look around you… godsend, oh, Paddy…

PADDY: Hey. Perfect weather up here in the mountains. Listen, if we could transplant this place to anywhere in America, there'd be nothing but resorts and gated communities and golf courses and capitalism at its finest. And you, Tom, what have you found the most difficult? Obviously not the weather.

TOM: …an accumulation of… the language, the culture, so… complicated… their stubbornness, they cling to their old ways, I don't know, everything. They don't accept me. They annoy me to no end. On certain days.

PADDY: Like today…

TOM: Sorry to say it.

PADDY: Sometimes, when you think you're here for everyone, for all the people, it's overwhelming.

TOM: Even with the perfect weather, Paddy?

PADDY: I was ready to ask for a transfer, take me back…

TOM: No, not you, Paddy, can't believe it, you, give up?

PADDY: Give me a tough inner-city neighborhood, anything but this. And then, one morning… went out to say mass… 5:15 am… the monsoon, pouring down rain… and Alois was already in the chapel. Had the altar ready, everything prepared. And it dawned on me… I'm here for Alois. For one person. At a time. It was a revelation. Tom. Once you realize that, it's wonderful. Which one person will it be tomorrow, or next week, or even, the next moment? The battle for Christ is won with small victories. This isn't the crusades, Tom. It's an accumulation of small victories.

TOM: I couldn't have stayed a week if it weren't for you, Paddy.

But I don't know if I was made for this. The seminary did not prepare me. It was all romance, the romance of the bush, snapshots in a newsletter, stories of adventure. The hard facts are, there are few who can muster up what it takes to do the job here. Even the pidgin language eludes me.

PADDY: Yes, I'm surprised at that. We should spend more time together, working on it. You'll catch on.

TOM: Tenkyu tru.

PADDY: Welcom tru.

Short pause. TOM searches for the right words.

TOM: I saw something today.

PADDY: What?

TOM: Something I shouldn't have.

PADDY: What was that?

TOM walks across the room for water, working up his nerve.

TOM: After the cycle broke down, after I cursed it, god forgive me, I sat and rested. For a long time. Wondered whether I should just start to hike back, and leave the bike there. Of course, I was too deep into the bush for that... I thought about so many things. Couldn't bring myself to pull off the housing and get my hands greasy, one more time. So I just sat there. Thinking... And then... I heard a noise.

SFX, OFF: A woman's voice again. Ohhhaaaaeee.

TOM: Thought it was a bird of paradise. Hoping it was. I do enjoy seeing them. So I was still as I could be.

SFX, OFF: A woman's voice again. Ohhhaaaaeee.

TOM: No, that's not a bird, that's... a human voice... a girl's... It came again, and again... High pitched... and soft... so soft... stepped off the path, just a few steps, holding my breath, actually. And... this young girl... a man on top of her... behind a tree... just their legs... mostly. Copulating. I stepped back. But I... I couldn't stop watching... I watched until they finished. Then... furiously went to work on the bike, making as much noise as I could. So they'd know I was there. They left. They never saw me.

PADDY: ...It is the only privacy they have, in the bush. As you know. We must give them their privacy... Sit down, Tom.

TOM: *He sits. With remorse.* It was sinful... to watch them... making love.

PADDY: If you took pleasure in it, yes. God has already forgiven you... It's their culture. The men live in one hut, the women in another. So the bush is their only choice... when they want to make love. The wives are faithful. The men not always. Ha. It's an uphill battle with that one, I tell you.

TOM: Paddy, you missed my point. I watched them. I could have turned my head away, but I didn't. It was sinful. It was dirty of me to just... watch... but I couldn't... turn away.

PADDY: Well... It's about time you saw how it's done, and what it's like. Don't beat yourself up about it. The most important thing was, do you know what it was?

TOM: I can't imagine.

PADDY: They didn't see you. You didn't embarrass them. Next time, if there is a next time, just look away. Find that bird of paradise. Go on about your business. No big deal. It happens. It's life. Ha, there wouldn't be life without it, now would there?

TOM: Paddy, I have to ask you, if you don't mind.

PADDY: I don't.

TOM: Do you find celibacy difficult?

PADDY: At times, yes. Or not as often, I should say. Actually, you being here has helped.

TOM: How so?

PADDY: Another celibate person. The Capuchins are a brotherhood. We support each other. I'm so glad you're here. Giving up the marriage union, the physical love… the attraction is…

TOM: *Jumping on a hidden thought.* Yes. The attraction is… tremendous… overwhelming.

PADDY: It's a beautiful thing, sex. But we've chosen celibacy, which is also beautiful, and a total commitment to Christ, to the priesthood, to our Capuchin brotherhood. Nothing could be more total, more complete, or, to me, more wonderful.

TOM: I find myself… thinking about it…

PADDY: Of course you do. We're sexual beings, all of us. You become a priest, that doesn't make you any less sexual. I was a man, first, long before I was ordained. Ordination didn't castrate me, huh? Now, there's an idea. *Laughs, but TOM doesn't.* Sorry. Look, the attraction will always be there, always, thank God. What would life be without it? But that's also what makes celibacy so complete, so wonderful… Any of this making sense to you?

TOM: Yes. And I believe it. And yet, I don't know…

PADDY: Let us pray for each other in this regard, every day. And discuss it whenever you want. Anytime, Tom.

TOM: Thank you, Paddy.

PADDY: If I make it to heaven, I have one question for God. Yes, about sex. God, why did you have to make it so attractive, so much fun? Couldn't you have made it, just a… a little bit of fun… Just enough to keep the races going… and then on to other things.

TOM: Yes, yes… why must we be like… like magnets that even through thick walls attract each other and get stuck together, impossible to pry apart. Why couldn't sex be…

PADDY: Yes, just a little less exciting… instead of…

TOM: … something that makes people lose their whole sense of being, lose their minds…

PADDY: …even their souls, huh?

TOM: …for that brief moment of absolute orgasm and total, TOTAL ecstasy…

PADDY: No need to get carried away, Tom…

TOM: Yes, carried away. That's it exactly, Paddy. Sometimes, the way women look at you here, I feel they're attracted to me. And I feel drawn to them… every so often. It's just there. And then I think, it's my imagination… It has become a torment…

PADDY: You're not imagining things. Tom. There are plenty out there who would like to claim you.

TOM: Don't tell me that.

PADDY: Why? Look, you're a handsome young man.

TOM: Please…

PADDY: You are. You're also a symbol of authority, which is even more mysterious to young women here, and they can be very attracted to it. Our white skin adds to the mystery, huh? For some, a waitman may even be a little erotic. As she would be for us, too… if we chose to fantasize. *Pauses, as he is tempted to fantasize.* So I try never to be alone with any young woman.

TOM: What about… Clare? She is here all the time.

PADDY: She comes and she goes. She's Clare. She cooks and she cleans. And she is very sweet. She doesn't come to me with fish eyes and ask to sit with me privately. Then I would say, let's step outside, and sit in the courtyard. I think maybe she has her heart set on Alois, but then again, so do I. Ha.

TOM: What?

PADDY: Alois is priest material. He could be the first from his tribe. The first Huli priest. Think what that would mean to his people. We must cultivate that in him if he shows the least interest.

TOM: Perhaps he could take my place. He'd do a better job.

PADDY: *Kindly.* Tom, stop it. Don't do this to yourself. Get your mind off it. And pray, we must pray about this. It will make you stronger.

TOM: Thank you for talking about it, Paddy. It's been on my mind.

PADDY: It helps me also, Tom. Ha... Celibacy? They just don't get it. Don't even have a word for it. Doesn't exist. Over thousands of years, this is how they survived. You take a mate, you have children, take another mate, have more children. So, perfectly normal for a girl to let you know that she is interested. But...

TOM: But... there's a but, thank God...

PADDY: It would be disastrous. If I had a moment of weakness, there is no turning back for her. She must marry me. No other man would want her. And, no dowry, no bridewealth, no pig, no kina shell. My life here would be over. And so would hers. It dawned on me as I looked at a beautiful young thing, who was looking at me with big, brown eyes, in a sort of wonder.

TOM: Good to know you're human, too, Paddy. I'm not alone...

PADDY: And neither am I.

CLARE enters.

CLARE: Pata, how you like kamu?

PADDY: Wonderful. They were... different, very tasty. How did you roast them?

CLARE: Chop chop sugar cane, small piece, put inside, roast slow like over gud fire.

PADDY: I'll add that recipe to my collection. Excellent.

CLARE: Tenkyu tru. Pata Tom, you no eat up?

TOM: I wasn't all that hungry. Very nice. But thank you.

CLARE: Is welcome yu, Pata Tom...

TOM admires her as she cleans the table.

PADDY: Have you seen Alois, Clare, in your travels?

CLARE: That Alois, always somewhere. Sometimes he just sit... luk. I tink... why? Alois, why yu lukluk? I say. Tsk tsk. That Alois.

PADDY: I'll find him. He promised to take me to SumiSami tomorrow. Do you know SumiSami?

CLARE: All Huli know SumiSami, Pata. Oh, ples masalai.

PADDY: Oh, a sacred place, oh, my. Ples masalai. I'm impressed.

CLARE: Why you go there, Pata, you in love? *Laughs.* Pata Paddy in love, oh my, what people say... Pata Paddy, tsk tsk tsk...

PADDY: Alois told me the story. It's fantastic, and I just have to see this... ples masalai... so... Alois said he would take me there. Tom, can you say the eight o'clock mass tomorrow morning, and stay near the mission? Have you any plans?

TOM: *Has been watching CLARE, distracted.* What's that? Tomorrow, yes, I'm here. Have a Catechist class, late morning, catch up on my correspondence. I'm here.

PADDY: I'll be back late afternoon sometime, ok?

PADDY and TOM stand.

Pata Tom?

TOM: Thank you Lord... for your continued faith in us and your help in everything we do... and your understanding of our human frailties... and... a special blessing on the gifted hands of your daughter Clare who created this... wonderful meal. Amen.

CLARE smiles at the mention of her name, blesses herself.

Perhaps the generator will have some juice by then and we can call for supplies. Do you mind if I order something from the market in Mendi?

PADDY: Well... ok, yes, of course. Just remember our budget, please.

TOM: I'll keep it simple, Paddy, honestly...

PADDY: It's just that...our stipend check from the diocese didn't arrive today.

TOM: It's always on time.

PADDY: Well, it probably arrived... but we didn't get it...

TOM: The rascals stole our mail, again. Paddy!

PADDY: I'm afraid so. Moses picked up the mail, had it in our canvas bag, set it down to get something from the jeep. He said he was just a moment...

TOM: *Burst of anger.* That Moses is irresponsible. You need to talk to him.

PADDY: We can't blame Moses. It's the rascals. I told Moses that from now on, we can't let the mail out of our sight.

TOM: The check from the Provincial office, news from home, important papers, I was expecting... something... now we'll never know... This is impossible...

PADDY: *Laughs.* If we could just get them to steal all the bills and all the bad news, then I think I'd even pay them to steal the mail... It will sort itself out...

TOM: God help us if I'm ever in charge here.

PADDY: God help us anyhow, whoever's in charge. If Alois comes in, tell him I'm out looking for him.

CLARE: I look down by riva, Pata. He go there, look in riva.

Tsk tsk tsk.

PADDY: Thank you, Claire…

PADDY exits.

Alone now, TOM watches CLARE as she cleans the table.

TOM: Clare, this SumiSami… what is it…? Why does Pata Paddy want to go there?

CLARE: *Stops, has to think about this.* I tink… he want go there because… he magic man… and SumiSami magic place.

TOM: Pata Paddy… How is he magic man?

CLARE: Everyone feel… help with Inglis… feel… gud… have someting… yu say, special… You feel too?

TOM: I would agree. A very special man.

CLARE: Ok, SumiSami… also… so special. No one go but Huli. I think Pata Paddy be na ba wan person not Huli go there. But… that Pata Paddy.

TOM: Tell me about this SumiSami… please…

TOM grows more infatuated with CLARE as her loveliness comes through her storytelling, her love of this poetic tale, her childlike belief and near rapture as she tells him about SumiSami. She walks about the room, takes a few steps closer to TOM until she is very close by the end of her tale.

SFX: Drums sneak in and punctuate her story.

CLARE: Oh, I don't know… yu no person who believe SumiSami, I don't know. Yu tink stori nating, maybe.

TOM: Why do you say that?

CLARE: Maybe yu laugh…

TOM: Maybe you're wrong. Why would I laugh? Is it a funny story?

CLARE: To yu, maybe.

TOM: Try me.

CLARE: Try yu?

TOM: Yes. Try. Test me. Tell me the story. See if I laugh. I'll bet I don't.

CLARE: Bet, what is bet?

TOM: What I'm trying to say, is… I would love to hear the story.

CLARE: *Laughs.* Love, yes, story of love.

TOM: Well, now, there you are. So… SumiSami? Please?

CLARE: Ok, yu want SumiSami.

> *CLARE comes to near where TOM is sitting, folds her hands, as if preparing for a recital, pauses, thinking of the best way to tell her story. She sits down across from TOM but eventually moves about as she herself gets caught up in the telling.*

CLARE: Many family time ago, many year, many people tell story, one to other, until Clare learn, so it tru, tru as can be. My mama say me, her mama say her, yu understand? And she take me there little girl. Ples masalai.

TOM: A sacred place.

CLARE: Gud pidgin, Pata Tom.

TOM: So?

CLARE: So… SumiSami… One time, far away in jungle, live Huli tribe, live beautiful girl, she so beautiful, she more beautiful than anyting. Also live young man. He see and he love, oh, so love. In pidgin, mangalim… want… so, so much, understand?

TOM: Mangalim. To want someone… so much.

CLARE: Yes, yes, never see girl so beautiful. She tru beautiful. *CLARE gestures to tell her story. It becomes a dance.* So beautiful, sun it shine from face, moon it shine from eyes, love it shine from smile, she tok, like soft wind, she walk, like beautiful bird, everyting she touch, like flower, she make everyting beautiful. She walk by, people smile, young men no can breathe. Shhhh. She tru beautiful. So beautiful, no man can say, marry me. Brave man, brave in fight, strong warrior, afraid say marry me. She tru beautiful. But one boy, he so in love, he see her and he know. Mangalim.

TOM: He must have her.

CLARE: Yes, yes. His name… SumiSami. So… one day, SumiSami, he go house in jungle. She live away from village. Live by self. He go, he tell her. I love you. I marry.

She laugh. Nice laugh. She say, yu SumiSami. He say, yes, I SumiSami. Yu know me? She laugh. SumiSami, you marry me, I only one. I make happy. So happy you can no dream. But I only one. Yu promise?

Oh, yes. He promise. Promise all day, all night… So, she listen… say, yes, I marry. Ohhh, he so happy. She happy, too. But she say him, I only one, must never touch other woman. No touch. One touch, so bad. So, so bad. So they marry, and oh, so happy. Her gaden, kamap bigpela. Kau kau, grow like elephant, coffee trees, bloom day, bloom night. People see, cannot believe. She magic. Have magic gaden. House, most beautiful. Everything, so… nam ba wan.

TOM: Nam ba wan. Best… you mean perfect, Clare, it was perfect.

CLARE: Yes. Perfect best. He happi man. No wok. She do all. Like Clare. *Laughs at her own joke.* He do nating. Just luk luk at her, beautiful. And, ok, make love, excuse me, Pata, most best love. Understand? She malum malum, yu say, so gud, so soft. She mangalim tru… make magic love, Pata…

TOM: Yes. I understand. She… mangalim tru…

CLARE: One day… is sing sing in village. So he say, I go sing sing. She say, ok, yu go, but what I say? No touch other woman. He laugh, he say, why touch, yu I love.

But she know sing sing, she know SumiSami, so... she tie vine on leg, long, long vine. No one see but her, rope i stop long leg, yu no en lukim, understand...? No can see?

TOM: An invisible rope...

CLARE: Yes, no visible rope, and he say... lookim yu bihain now, go sing sing. So, at sing sing, all happy, he see friends, he see family, he see pretty girl. Many pretty girl. At sing sing, all dancing. Young men do fight dance. Young mamas do baby dance. Old men do dance for hunt wild pig. Old women do cassowary dance. All dance, ok? One dance, all girl, all boy, dance to meet boy, girl, understand?

TOM: Yes, a dance to meet someone...

SFX: *Drums begin to "dance."*

CLARE: So happi, happi dance. SumiSami. He laugh, he chew buai nut, he more happi. Maybe, too happi. All time, rope i stop on leg, yu no ken lookim. So, dance with young girl, young boy, SumiSami watch. But ... so happi he jump up, what he do, he dance with girl. He no touch. He dance. But she so close, so close... *CLARE gets closer to TOM.* She dance. She dance...

Dances up to TOM. He reach over... He take hand...
He touch.

She takes his hand, pulls him toward her, slowly, gently, walking backwards, looking into his eyes, acting out the story. TOM is taken by her.

Oh, my, SumiSami feel someting pull leg. Pull and pull. Pull him from girl, from dance, from sing sing. SumiSami make loud, say help, help, but people know... magic... they watch... watch pull him into jungle.

All way back, she pull him. Back, to home, to gaden...
But... she no there. He see gaden. All dying. Kau kau, all dying. House, now sluppy. He look for her, no find. Oh, no. SumiSami, he sit, he cry. He call for her... but nating. He say

he sorry. But nating. So sad. He say he die. Now… far away, he hear… "SumiSami, SumiSami…" She call name. He get up, he stop cry, he go find… "SumiSami…. SumiSami…" He happi now, he run through jungle… "SumiSami… SumiSami…" Go more fast. Then, he see… but she no girl, she now bird of paradise, most beautiful bird ever see. She call him… "SumiSami… SumiSami…" He run. He long long with love. He so crazy. He reach out. She fly up on tree. He reach out. But… tree on high rock, so high up, so far down, understand?

TOM: It was a cliff. The edge of a cliff.

CLARE: He so close, he try touch, and… "SumiSami." …he fall. Down, down down… To rocks. "SumiSami… SumiSami." He die… for love… bottom rocks. SumiSami…

People in village, they look for him long time, find him… bottom rocks. They know… he die for love… love her so much.

TOM: For her… magalim tru…

CLARE: Yes. Magic love, so much… *Shyly, but sensuously.* … malgalim tru.

They are close, look into each other's eyes. Now… Huli go there, look for bones. Call it SumiSami. Find small bone… good luck. Some find, but I tink maybe… bone belong cassowary, bird of paradise… Laughs.

…Boy, girl in love go there, find bone good luck, for marry. Some day, I marry. I find maliraim, someday. Now…

Laughs. …Pata Paddy go there with Alois, you tink he in love? Ha… So… SumiSami. You no laugh, Pata Tom… tenkyu tru.

TOM: It is a beautiful story, Clare.

CLARE: So hepi yu laik, I tink, SumiSami maybe not yu stori, but yu laikim dispela stori.

TOM: You tell it beautifully.

CLARE: Oh, no, Inglis no so good.

TOM: My pidgin not so good. Clare… would you like some help with your English?

CLARE: Need help, Pata. I want… tok gud Ingis.

TOM: I can help you. And you can help me with tok pison. Can you teach me pidgin?

CLARE: Tok pison easy. Inglis no so easy.

TOM: Tomorrow morning, come here, and I will help you.

CLARE: Oh, I come moning. You help plis?

TOM: Yes. I will help you.

CLARE: Tenkyu tru. So much I tenk you. Clare smile all night.

TOM: You have a beautiful smile.

CLARE: Ohhh.

TOM: Welcom yu. Tomorrow, after breakfast.

CLARE: Moning time. So nice. Pata Tom, yu gudpela.

A pause, they smile at the prospect of tomorrow morning. TOM reaches out his hand to hers. CLARE takes it, smiling.

TOM: Thank you for SumiSami, Clare.

It's a moment. CLARE slowly withdraws her hand.

CLARE: Finish, now, Pata, I go.

TOM: Tomorrow morning, then.

CLARE: Yu so kind, yu give this me. Moning time.

TOM: Yes… Well…

An awkward moment as CLARE is ready to leave and neither of them want that. Then CLARE leaves quickly with a burst of laughter.

CLARE: So hepi. Smile all night… lukim yu tomora, Pata.

TOM: Yes… Good-by… I… tomorrow…

CLARE exits.

TOM watches her leave.

Lights down.

Act One
Scene Five

Lights up on ALOIS, sitting on his haunches, gazing into the "river." He has put away his pad and pencil.

PADDY enters, watches him for a moment.

PADDY: Good evening, Alois.

ALOIS: Pata Paddy, hello. You frighten me.

PADDY: You were lost in thought.

ALOIS: Yes…

PADDY: Maybe you see something in the water?

ALOIS: I see so much in the water, works a spell on you, does it not.

PADDY: Yes. It is hypnotizing.

ALOIS: Yes, that is the word.

PADDY: But what do you see?

ALOIS: Sometimes, nothing. Sometimes, so much. You can see your life in the river, Pata Paddy.

PADDY: Each day we wash away in the current, and each day we begin anew. I wonder, is this river big enough for our lives, so much is happening…

ALOIS: Sometimes I want to go down the Wagie river with my life, just to see where I will go…

PADDY: And where would you go?

ALOIS: It doesn't matter. To another place. To a big city. To Port Moresby. To Australia. New Zealand. Maybe even to the America you talk about, you love so much.

PADDY: You don't want to leave now, do you? Our day of independence is here. This is the time to be in Papua New Guinea, for young people like you.

ALOIS: I do think about that. I want to be part of it. But here, in the bush, nothing will change. In the big cities, in Madang, in Goroka, in Port Moresby, many changes. But in this Huli village, no. They don't understand, yet, what it means.

PADDY: Moses doesn't want to talk about it. I asked him, he says… independunce samting nating. I asked Clare, she has already forgotten.

ALOIS: *Laughs.* Moses, he is afraid all the helicopters and telephones will come, there will be no more sing sings, no more Huli, no more pig kills, no more painting faces yellow, no more spears and penis gourds. But he is Moses. And Clare… She is… just happy here… so happy. Clare is… Clare. She loves… wherever she is… She brings her smile.

PADDY: I am excited for the people.

ALOIS: I worry for the people. I am afraid the rascals who steal the mail and the gasoline will now also steal the government.

PADDY: You are right to worry. But there must be a beginning, and a beginning is always exciting, Alois.

ALOIS: Ha. This is my Pata Paddy, all right. Always the same. It is why my people love you.

PADDY: You are very kind.

ALOIS: *Throws another pebble into the river.* And you are Pata Paddy. And yes, this independence. It is exciting. I see so many new things. I see the children. They are walking to a new school, one with a tin roof and windows. I see the old people go to a hospital for medicine. I see a child becomes a doctor. I see a road that takes our coffee and sweet potato and sugarcane to Port Moresby. I see a road all the way to Australia.

PADDY: I see the Huli sharing their land. I see people come from Australia and Indonesia to learn from Papua New Gunea. I see people discussing political candidates and I see them voting, for the first time, yes, for their new president.

ALOIS: Ha. This river is getting crowded, Pata. We need a bigger river.

PADDY: Yes, a bigger river, let us pray for a bigger river… Alois, you haven't forgotten about tomorrow? And your promise last week? To take me to SumiSami?

ALOIS: Oh, yes. I will take you. That's what I was thinking of, really.

PADDY: So, SumiSami is who you saw in the water, huh?

ALOIS: Yes. Well… not exactly.

PADDY: Do you not want to go? We can make it another time.

ALOIS: No, tomorrow is the day. We'll go if you like.

PADDY: You don't seem as excited as when you told me the story of SumiSami. Your eyes were alive and you were smiling. Where is that smile?

ALOIS: Sometimes you see too much, Pata. I'm happy to take you, to share one more Huli story, and this is a special one.

PADDY: It's just that…

ALOIS: It's just that… as I was sitting here… I was thinking of…

PADDY: Clare…

ALOIS: You can see inside me.

PADDY: No, I can see outside you. In your eyes.

ALOIS: Once I asked Clare to go with me to SumiSami… She laughed… said I was foolish to think that she would go there with me. I did not think it was so foolish.

PADDY: So, Clare was who you were looking at in the water, huh? The river reveals so much.

ALOIS: Yes…

PADDY: And I was thinking… Clare had her eye on you…

ALOIS: No. It is my eye on Clare. I wish she were going with me tomorrow, I have to say it.

PADDY: Alois… I didn't know you cared for her so much.

ALOIS: Do you think me foolish?

PADDY: Foolish? …You remember the story of St. Francis? He was so in love with life, with his God, with his brothers, with the birds and animals and all around him, many people called him a fool. He said he was God's fool. I pray every day for that kind of foolish love. Alois, look at me… If you love someone, it is never foolish.

ALOIS: *Bright and cheerful.* Ok, Pata Paddy… SumiSami! …And you will be… astonished. Are you ready for a long hike?

PADDY: Let's leave at dawn. I will pack some fruit and bread in my bilum.

ALOIS: Just the bread. I know where there is wonderful mango and banana on the way. Moses tells me it is where the beautiful maiden had her magic "gaden," so we will eat SumiSami's fruit, too. Not many can say that.

PADDY: Tomorrow, then.

ALOIS: *Imitating the maiden.* SumiSami… SumiSami…

PADDY: And we will look for one of SumiSami's bones…

ALOIS: No, we will find a bone… for you… for good luck… Ok? *Puts out his hand.*

PADDY: *Grasping it with both of his.* Ok. Tomorrow, first light?

ALOIS: We can meet here.

PADDY: *Starts to leave.* Thank you, Alois. Coming up?

ALOIS: I think I will look into the river somewhat longer…

PADDY: Have a good night, then…

ALOIS: Good night, Pata.

PADDY starts to exit, looks back at ALOIS, smiles at him and exits.

After a moment, MOSES enters. He has been watching them. He has a machete and long piece of sugarcane. He approaches ALOIS.

ALOIS: That was a quick trip to Mendi for petrol, too quick.

MOSES: I find petrol. Will give it to Pata… in morning.

MOSES sits on his haunches, cuts a sliver of the sugar cane with his machete, gives it to ALOIS, and slices another for himself. Chews it as he talks.

ALOIS: You should give it to him tonight.

MOSES: Moning. Soon enough.

ALOIS: The Rewani man… everyone is talking…

MOSES: Everyone talking. Oli tok tok nating…

ALOIS: I see you have another bone for your collection… *Nods his head to MOSES' necklace.*

MOSES: This is Huli way… everything be made right… always…

ALOIS: It is all wrong… We are Christian, Moses…

MOSES: Huli first, always first… Christian is to… wok, have job, help Pata…

ALOIS: No more job if he finds out about this business… I told you not to…

MOSES: Pata Paddy I no sa-ve…

ALOIS: God knows. God sa-ve.

MOSES: *A scornful laugh.* God knows. Moses knows. You take Pata Paddy to SumiSami.

ALOIS: *Shakes his head, disappointed.* You were listening? … Tomorrow morning, yes.

MOSES: Not right. Not Huli. Not even Pata Paddy.

ALOIS: He is more Huli than my own family. He loves Huli. I take him to SumiSami. *Laughs.* Pata Paddy. Huli.

MOSES: *Angry.* He not Huli. He magic man, all right, but he not Huli. He waitman. Not Huli! Some things only Huli. Some people only Huli.

ALOIS: Some things only Christian. Some things only Huli. Some things this. Some things that. We are changing, Moses. We have to be one, as brothers. Like St. Francis. Have you forgotten what happens in a few days?

MOSES: Nating happens.

ALOIS: Our independence. We are a free country. No more ask the Australians, ask for this, ask for that, live by their laws. We will make our own laws. One tribe, one country.

MOSES: *Anger rises.* Never one tribe, one country. Always Huli. My papa, you papa, everyone. Who care about us, live in jungle… make our way, help each other. No one. Get sick, nobody come. Die, who bury? Only Huli help Huli.

ALOIS: No, Pata Paddy help Huli. Always here for us. You get sick, he has a pill for you… say yes… You get malaria last year, who gives you pills? You forget? Our independence will happen, old ways will change, new ways will come, and Huli… *Points to his heart.* Huli will always be here. I love Huli.

They clasp hands and forearms.

MOSES: No take Pata Paddy to SumiSami. Bad magic, Alois. Very bad magic.

ALOIS: Moses. It is ok. Tomorrow I will take him. Moning time. We will look for the bones. We will find the bones. Maybe… maybe he will wear it with his cross. Ha. You have your bones. He has his cross. Maybe… maybe we should make a cross out of SumiSami's bones. Ha. Then what do you think? *For Moses.*

MOSES: I teach all I know about Huli, and you do this?

ALOIS: Moses, this is Pata Paddy…

MOSES and ALOIS have a heated exchange in pidgin, a short burst, but very angry, especially Moses. It resolves quickly.

MOSES: Huli, pasim bilong yumi em olsem! (Huli, this is how we do things!)

ALOIS: Lotru wed okum ily-o! (Real law is coming!)

MOSES: Bulsit! Payback tru wed! (Rubbish! Payback is true law!)

ALOIS: Ekepu gvman okum ilyi-oi! (New government is coming!)

MOSES: Ekep ily mada inap, inap! (Now that's enough, enough!)

ALOIS: *Calmly.* Inap, you are right, inap. *His anger changes to resolve.* You will see the respect Pata Paddy has for SumiSami, for Huli, how he will talk about it, how he will share it, how he loves all of us, all the Huli. How he loves you, Moses. Yes, how he loves you.

ALOIS exits.

After a beat, MOSES holds his machete over his head with both hands, then slams the machete into the piece of sugarcane, as if severing someone's limb.

MOSES: ARRGGGGGGGGG!

Go to black.

End of Act I.

Act Two
Scene One

The next morning. Inside the mission.

SFX: Drums, soft, early morning, waking up.

PATA TOM reading from his breviary, pacing. He stops, not able to concentrate, snaps it shut, places it on the table, bends slightly over it, as if in some pain. His is agonizing. He makes the sign of the cross, takes a deep breath.

TOM: *A whisper.* God... My God...

CLARE enters.

She is tentative, waits for a moment to interrupt. She wears a dress, brightly colored, crisp, a step up from the day before. She is fresh and bright. She doesn't want to startle TOM, but she does.

CLARE: Moning, Pata Tom...

TOM: Oh... Moning, Clare...

CLARE: You want breakfast, Pata?

TOM: Just had some cereal. Do you care for some?

CLARE: No. Eat prut my breakfast... So...

TOM: So...

CLARE: So... moning... afta breakfast time...

TOM: Yes, this is after breakfast...

CLARE: You say, come moning, you help Inglis.

TOM: Yes, I said that, I will help with your English. And you will help with my pidgin.

CLARE: Inglis more hard, so more words, so more... Make laugh.

TOM: You laugh easily.

CLARE: Laugh easy. What hard, laugh? Inglis hard. Laugh easy. *Laughs.* See...

TOM: Clare, perhaps... it would be best to wait for Pata Paddy... then the three of us... to teach English...

CLARE: Sit wait long time, Pata Paddy go SumiSami with Alois. Wait all day. *Sits down, laughs.* Ok. We wait.

TOM: Nononono... What I mean is... the two of us...

CLARE: Mi yu.

TOM: Yes... me, you... alone here. Perhaps...

CLARE: No alone. *CLARE gets up, walks around.* Tari wake up. Birds wake up. Bandicoot wake up. Moses fix machine. Tap tap tap. All Tari make music. Moning music. You hear, Pata Tom?

TOM: No, I don't hear, Clare, hear what?

CLARE: Listen... shhhh....

TOM: What?

CLARE: Shhhh.

CLARE puts her hand up to his mouth, holds it there for a few seconds.

SFX: Drums imitate birds, early morning sounds.

CLARE: Yes? ...You hear now?

TOM: I... I don't know...

CLARE: Yes...?

TOM: I... think so, I'm not sure...

CLARE: Most beautiful sound, moning music. Most reason live here. Wake up. Hear moning sounds long time. Pata Tom, someday, you hear moning music you be happi.

TOM: I hope so, Clare. I don't know... Clare, did you smile all night?

CLARE: Sleep all night.

TOM: You said, last night, when you thought about the lesson today, you would smile all night.

CLARE: Yes. All night... Smile now.

TOM: Yes. Well... let's get started, shall we?

CLARE: Ok. Tok gud Inglis bilong me, em i strait, ok?

TOM: That's as good a place to begin as ny.

They sit across from each other. CLARE leans in, smiling at him, and he at first leans back, a little intimidated.

TOM: To begin with...

CLARE: Start, yes?

TOM: Yes, start, begin, same thing. Same meaning. To start with...

CLARE: Begin, yes?

TOM: Yes, the same.

CLARE: So fun to learn.

TOM: So MUCH fun to learn. Clare, you have to begin using verbs, prepositions, adjectives and conjunctions.

CLARE just stares at TOM and smiles.

TOM: Never mind.

CLARE: Never... mind... so fun to learn...

TOM: *Teaching, now. he speaks slowly.* It is going to be so much fun to learn.

CLARE: Never mind.

TOM: Not... much fun to learn... It is going to be... say it...It is going to be...

CLARE: It going to be…

TOM: It IS going to be…

CLARE: Yes. IS going to be.

TOM: So much fun to learn.

CLARE: So much fun to learn.

TOM: Now the whole thing. It is going to be so much fun to learn.

CLARE: Going to be… SO much fun to learn.

TOM: No…

CLARE: No?

TOM: IT IS going to be… SO much fun to learn.

CLARE: IT IS going to be… SO much fun to learn.

TOM: Yes. Yes. Wonderful. That's it.

CLARE: IT IS going to be… SO much fun to learn. IT IS going to be… SO much fun to learn. *She makes it into a song.* IT IS going to be… SO much fun to learn. IT IS going to be… SO much fun to learn. IT IS going to be…

TOM: Ok, ok, that's it. You have it. Do you see the difference?

CLARE: *Look at him sweetly.* I see… beard. Have nice beard.

TOM: You have A nice beard. A nice beard.

CLARE: No me, yu. Ha. Yu have nice beard.

TOM: A… nice beard. Always put the A before the adjective or noun, and make a complete sentence. *She just smiles at him.* Ok, just remember this. A… nice beard. Say it.

CLARE: A… nice beard.

TOM: A… beautiful morning.

CLARE: A… beautiful moning.

TOM: A… beautiful MORNing. Not MONing. Speak English, not tok pisin.

CLARE: A… beautiful MORNing.

TOM: Yes. Excellent.

CLARE: A nice beard. A beautiful MORNing.

TOM: A pretty blouse.

CLARE: Pata Tom, tenk yu tru.

TOM: Say it. A pretty blouse.

CLARE: A pretty blouse. A nice beard. A beautiful MORNing.

TOM: That's very good.

CLARE: *Dances as she speaks.* A pretty blouse. A nice beard. A beautiful MORNing. A big table. A little chair. A dirty sink. A hot stove. A sluppy floor. A big cross.

SFX: Drums punctuate her dance.

TOM enjoys her little romp, as she turns it into a playful dance, twirling around. He laughs at her.

CLARE: …A little cup. A big book. A funny Pata. A ringy bell. A nice kaukau. A big window. A pretty sky. A hepi Clare.

TOM: A happy dance. A pretty Clare.

CLARE dances over to TOM. He is taken by her dance.

TOM: A wonderful morning.

CLARE: A nice Pata Tom.

TOM: A pretty Clare. *About to touch her face, but stops.* Clare, that was a beautiful story last night. SumiSami. You told it… with great affection. With love. With such honesty. I thought about you… I mean, I thought about the story, lying in bed.

CLARE: Tell yu tru... tok bilong yu? ...im i stret? ...mi tink... SumiSami... mi tink, Pata Tom... mi tink... Pata Tom, mi laikim Pata Tom... Pata Tom... im Pata, mi Clare... mi tink, long wanem Pata Tom im no hepi? ...im wonem im no hepi? ...Mi tink... mi makin im hepi... Mi makin im smile.... im makin me hepi...

TOM: I think about your smile. And I smile.

CLARE: I tink... why Pata Tom no hepi?

TOM: Why do you think I'm not happy?

CLARE: That Pata Paddy, he hepi. He smile, he sing, he laugh...

TOM: He is a great man.

CLARE: Yes. All love Pata Paddy.

TOM: Yes, that is so true. We all love Pata Paddy... Clare... What do people think of me, your people?

CLARE: Oh... Pata Tom...

TOM: Please. What do they say?

CLARE: Say... you no like Huli... you no like Tari. I say... Pata Tom... he no hepi... Some day, I tink, he hepi... then... he like. This place. Be hepi... then he like... Why... Pata Tom... you no like?

TOM: I come from such a different place. America is so different, Clare, you could never imagine.

CLARE: I magine?

TOM: In your mind, imagine, think about it, make a picture, in your mind, as you think it might be...

CLARE: Ok... ating (I think) ...many people... many waitman... very busy... wok wok wok... tok nice Inglis... many big town... city... too much... much... big... Port Moresby, I go one time... no more... Push push push... many raskols... take from you... Alois, he want go, want live there, want... wok, wok, wok... No me... No Clare... I tink... No me... Tari my home... I laik Tari...

TOM: Tari is beautiful... I do love the birds... the jungle, well, sometimes... the people... a mystery to me...

CLARE: Pata Tom, mi mama say, one time say, Clare no forget... be hepi? Laik one ting... laik, understand? Love. Little ting. Love... sky. Then, love one more ting. Love... bird. Then, one more... love flower... then, one more... then, one more... then one day, see how much you love, and you hepi. So, lose one hepi ting, have other hepi ting. Bird fly away, you hepi. Flower die, you hepi. Sky there. New bird come. Moning come. Moning music come. You understand?

TOM: Very wise, your mother. Many little happy things. Perhaps that is the secret. I try to find the happy things here, but...

CLARE: No. No no no... Pata Tom, one hepi ting. One only... Begin... One hepi ting.

TOM: One happy thing... all right, one happy thing... I found it...

CLARE: Ok, one hepi ting... What is?

TOM: You, Clare. You are... my one happy thing, so happy.
Takes her hand.

CLARE: Yes. I hepi. Ok. I hepi ting... for Pata Tom.

TOM: Yes. My one happy thing.

CLARE: One hepi ting Pata Tom...

TOM: Yes...

CLARE: Close eye, Pata Tom.

TOM closes his eyes. Perhaps CLARE touches them with her finger to help. Then she kisses him, sweetly, gently, slowly. TOM is immovable. CLARE pulls away and waits for him to open his eyes. TOM is stunned, completely taken by her.

CLARE: Now, two hepi ting.

TOM: Yes, now… two happy things.

CLARE: Pata Tom smile. One more hepi ting…

TOM: One more happy thing, please… *He kisses her, gently.*

CLARE: Pata Tom hepi now…

TOM: One more happy thing…

He is suddenly aggressive, tries to kiss her, but she backs away, resistant, but smiling as he pursues her.

CLARE: *Laughs.* No, too many hepi ting.

TOM: One more happy thing…

TOM catches her against the wall, kisses her. She first accepts, then pushes him away.

CLARE: No here… no here… inap… inap… Moses come… Pata!

She breaks away, goes to the sink, where she pauses. TOM does not pursue her, but turns to her.

TOM: Where, then? Where?

CLARE: No here. Moses come.

TOM: Take me to SumiSami.

CLARE: SumiSami…

TOM: Yes…

CLARE: *The very thought scares her, and delights her.* SumiSami…

TOM turns slightly away, their backs to each other.

MOSES enters.

MOSES: Moning, Pata.

TOM: Moning, Moses.

MOSES looks at them, senses their tenseness.

MOSES: Moning, Clare.

CLARE: Dishes done, wash clothes. Sluppy, so sluppy. Tsk tsk tsk. *As she exits, pauses at the door.* For Inglis lesson, Pata Tom, THANK yu tru. MORNing, Moses.

CLARE exits.

TOM has not moved. MOSES looks at him suspiciously.

MOSES: Yu have wok for Moses?

TOM picks up his breviary, is very business-like with MOSES.

TOM: Didn't Pata Paddy leave you a list?

MOSES: Pata go SumiSami. With Alois.

TOM: Well, did he leave you a list?

MOSES: Bad magic, go SumiSami.

TOM: *A wisp of anger.* Bad Magic, good magic, what is it with you? No magic, Moses, NO magic, when are you going to learn that? The Christian way is not magic, it is faith. Faith in Jesus. And redemption. Saving your soul. It's not magic.

MOSES: Yu have wok for Moses? Yu have lista?

TOM: Yes, I have WOK for Moses. I have LISTA. Two things. First, I want locks on the petrol. I want two locks. That generator is never to go without petrol again. Never. That is your responsibility. Do you understand?

MOSES: Moses lokup. You say two thing.

TOM gets closer, almost in his face, angry.

TOM: When you pick up the mail, and get this straight… Never, NEVER, leave the mail alone. It never leaves your sight. Never. The mail gets stolen again, you lose your job, you understand?

MOSES: Yes, understand. Gud Inglis lesson. Moses fixim.

SFX: Drums accentuate the action, anger of the moment.

MOSES exits.

TOM picks up his breviary, holds it tightly to his chest, then slams it on the table.

Go to black.

SFX: Drums segue to next scene. The jungle. Distant feel.

Act Two
Scene Two

PADDY and ALOIS in the jungle. They are dressed for hiking. PADDY is especially colorful. A leprechaun. Stopping to rest, they pass a canteen of water to each other.

PADDY: How much further, Alois?

ALOIS: Ha, Pata Paddy is tired already. We have only been gone for two hours..

PADDY: I'll out-hike you any day, Alois. This is my first love, hiking in the jungle. I was born hiking…

ALOIS: Ha. So, now they have jungles in this Pittsburgh in Pennsylvania, U S of A?

PADDY: They have huge forests, thick with trees, wonderful hills.

ALOIS: You miss that, you are homesick?

PADDY: Not anymore. I love the highlands. This is my home, now. God's country, you could say.

ALOIS: Moses would correct you. He would say this is Huli country. Moses… He was so angry last night.

PADDY: Angry about what? Why?

ALOIS: Angry with me, with you. So angry he worries me.

PADDY: I have only seen Moses angry once, when that young woman hung herself from the Wagie bridge. Do you remember?

ALOIS: Everyone saw his anger, the payback in his eyes. It was frightening… even other Huli, they backed away from him on that day.

PADDY: Is the payback in his eyes, still?

ALOIS: Always. It is in his heart. It is the Huli way. I try to talk to him, but, no use.

PADDY: There are so many good things about Moses. I suspect all these new Christian ideas are so difficult for him… to blend into the Huli culture. That is why I like having him around. Helps me to understand that. We must be patient, I think.

ALOIS: Patience is Papuan, Pata Paddy. My people can wait forever, and life continues. Even payback is patience. The anger sits inside, and then one day it bursts out like the tongue of a snake, and then retreats as if nothing happened. We must be careful at all times.

PADDY: So Moses is angry about Pata Paddy… going to SumiSami?

ALOIS: Oh, yes, how clever you are.

PADDY: The irony is, I plan to use SumiSami to show our people that I respect their culture and love their stories. Hey. Alois. I will preach about today and use SumiSami, huh? To show my love for Huli. Moses will understand that. Besides, this is an adventure, and one should never turn away from an adventure.

ALOIS: Wait until you see SumiSami, you never see anything like it, never in your life.

PADDY: Alois… was Moses involved with the Rewani man, the one who was murdered… was he connected to the payback?

ALOIS: You know about that?

PADDY: I'm not accusing, but the thought struck me last night when Pata Tom told me what happened…

ALOIS: Too many questions, Pata Paddy. No more, today is for SumiSami.

PADDY: I need to know. Moses may need my help. I want to help him…

ALOIS: Listen…

PADDY: What?

SFX: Drums, a distant sound.

ALOIS: Shhhh… SumiSami… SumiSami…

ALOIS runs off, laughing, PADDY runs after him.

PADDY: You can't lose me. Hey, I was born hiking…

SFX: Drums up, playfully, as PADDY runs off.

Go to black.

Act Two
Scene Three

Outside mission, later that morning.

Moses on his haunches, sharpening his machete with a stone. He is deliberate, with long strokes, with a rhythm, like a warrior preparing for battle.

SFX: Drums blend with the sound of the stone on metal, build and then fade as CLARE enters.

CLARE enters, carries a basket of clean wash, stops and turns when MOSES speaks to her.

MOSES: Pata Tom givim list long yu?

CLARE: Ples, tok Inglis, Moses

MOSES: *Laughs.* Planti wok bilong yumi tufela. Pata Tom give you list, huh, wash clothes, scrub floor, cook food…

CLARE: Make own list, nobody give.

MOSES: That Pata Tom, he man no gut. I decide. He trabelman.

CLARE puts her clothes down.

CLARE: Pata Tom gudman. He try hard. He miss home. He skulim mi, tisim Clare Inglis.

MOSES: He no like Huli. He go home. Best for him.

CLARE: No, Pata Tom need help. Need time. Huli way sometimes… hard.

CLARE goes up to MOSES from behind, puts her hands tenderly on his shoulder as she asks a favor.

CLARE: Moses, you help Pata Tom. Ok, Moses?

MOSES: Moses help Clare. Pata Tom, got planti problem. No like Huli.

CLARE: You helpim Pata Tom… for Clare.

MOSES: Why for Clare? Why you ask this?

CLARE: He gutpela. Nice to Clare. Tisim Inglis.

MOSES: Tok Inglis all day. Still Huli, Clare. Always Huli.

CLARE: Ok. But Clare laik Inglis.

MOSES: Alois tisim Inglis better.

CLARE: That Alois. He want go city. Alois look in riva. Have riva dreams. No. Clare, one touch Alois, he long long. That Alois. Tsk Tsk.

MOSES: Clare make all men crazy, one touch.

CLARE: *Still massaging his shoulder, teasing.* So, Moses, you crazy now?

MOSES: Too old now. Young men go crazy. Old men go home, go sleep.

CLARE: Moses, you helpim Pata Tom?

MOSES: Moses helpim Clare. You stay careful, understand? Yu lukaut.

CLARE: Ok, I lukaut. You helpim Pata Tom.

MOSES: I fixim petrol, fixim mail, fixim machine. Easy for Moses. Ahh, some things not so easy fixim. Pata Tom. Got planti problem.

CLARE: No, he need helpim. Need understand.

MOSES: Pata Tom switheart? Need touch?

CLARE: *Pulls away quickly, annoyed.* No. Need helpim. You long long, Moses. *Picks up her basket to leave.*

MOSES: *Points machete at her to make his point.* No when I say… you careful. Pata Tom tisim Inglis. Moses tism… you Huli.

CLARE: Yu long long olpela, Moses.

MOSES: *Laughs.* Plis, tok Inglis, Clare.

CLARE: You crazy old man!

    CLARE exits.

    SFX: Drums and MOSES sharpening his machete, then face.

    Go to black.

Act Two
Scene Four

The jungle.

ALOIS, in front of PADDY, stops and motions for PADDY to stop.

ALOIS: Ok, we stop here.

PADDY: Let's keep going, Alois, I can't wait.

ALOIS: Close your eyes, Pata...

PADDY: We're here? Ok. Wonderful.

PADDY takes a few steps forward, ALOIS stops him.

ALOIS: No, no, close your eyes, Pata.

PADDY: Oh, c'mon, Alois. Been hiking for hours.

ALOIS: Close your eyes, I insist.

PADDY: Both of them?

ALOIS: Both, you rascal. Good. Ok, this way.

PADDY closes his eyes, ALOIS takes his hand and leads him a few more steps to center, to the "edge" of the cliff.

ALOIS: Ok, open your eyes.

PADDY: *Opens his eyes, is stunned, amazed.* Oh, my. Wow. Alois...

ALOIS: SumiSami.

PADDY: Magnificent. Just... incredible.

ALOIS: Yes, it is all that.

PADDY: In all my travels, never... never seen a place so utterly... inspiring. One of God's wonders, truly. My heart is pounding.

ALOIS: You are the first white man, I think, to see this place. SumiSami.

PADDY: *Takes a step or two forward, closer to the edge.* Has to be... over five hundred meters to the bottom.

ALOIS: Careful. One step back, please. We don't want lovers looking for Pata Paddy's bones.

PADDY: A long ways down. You'd fall for days... Alois, a chill is going up my spine... almost... frightening. Has anyone else... ever died here?

ALOIS: Only SumiSami, I think. So many years ago. Who knows? There's the Bird of Paradise tree, see, where SumiSami reached out to his beautiful wife, and fell off the edge. His bones are below. Shall we go look?

PADDY: In a moment. *Sits down by the edge.* Can't take it all in. Thank you, Alois, I'll never forget this, the first time, no matter how many times I return. And I will come back, for sure.

ALOIS: Yes, it calls to you, does it not? I come by myself, sometimes. One time, I wrote a poem, sitting here. When I thought of all the love... and the broken love... that is here.

PADDY: I'd like to hear it. Please.

ALOIS: It is just a thought.

PADDY: Please.

ALOIS: *Sitting down.* Another time. Better just sit and enjoy.

PADDY: Alois, I feel badly for you.

ALOIS: Why would you say that, look how beautiful this is...

PADDY: I do. You wanted to bring Clare here, not a tired old priest with an ugly beard.

ALOIS: *Laughs.* Yes… that beard is truly ugly… Oh, I asked Clare, but… she is not ready, yet. She knows, if she comes here with me, she will marry me. And perhaps she is not ready yet. I will wait until she is.

PADDY: Does she know how much you love her? Have you ever told her?

ALOIS: I try… But the words twist around my tongue and come out like a kakatu's. I can't blame her. I tell her about my dreams, and hope she wants to be part of them, as she is in mine, but… she just laughs… And then gets angry… and then she laughs. Oh, I love her laugh…

PADDY: Well, remember… patience is Papuan? Huh?

ALOIS: Yes, but… it is difficult.

PADDY: You should not wait a moment longer.

ALOIS: What are you saying?

PADDY: Listen. I'm no expert on love. Except that I have felt Christ's love since I was a child. A love I want to share. To tell the world about. Well, this part of the world. That's why I became a Capuchin. And why I'm sitting here with you… a place that is so… I tell you, this place sinks into my soul… *Reverently* …SumiSami…

ALOIS: I wish I knew what you are saying…

PADDY: I'm saying… You have to preach your own gospel of love… to Clare. You have to tell her you love her. Don't you want her to know? Don't you want the world to know?

ALOIS: Clare would be enough. The world can wait.

PADDY: Then you must tell her. Find a way. You want her to lie on her mat at night and think about you. As you think about her. You have heard at mass the readings of St. Paul. Love is patient. Love is kind. And the three virtues…

ALOIS: …faith, hope and love. And the greatest of these is love. Without love, it is like a bell ringing in the night, that no one hears.

PADDY: Without love, it is a dream that drowns in the river, and you are a dreamer, Alois. Don't let this dream vanish. You will wake up some day and it is gone. No matter what happens in life, if you have a great love, it rises above all. Carries you in its arms.

ALOIS: Pata Paddy, you are most extraordinary. You must have a heart with eyes and ears attached.

PADDY: Now, why do you say that?

ALOIS: That is what my poem reflects upon. Did you steal my poem from my head?

PADDY: Share it with me.

ALOIS: I don't know…

PADDY: Please.

ALOIS: *Takes the poem from his pocket.* "My Love Has Wings." That is my title.

PADDY: Yes, yes…

ALOIS: "The morning has it's mist and dew
The sunshine has it's sky,
The evening has it's moon and stars
But the bird of love can fly.

The mountains have their flowing streams,
The valleys have their sighs,
The rivers have their hidden dreams,
But the bird of love can fly.

Whatever path my life may go
Whatever life the Lord may bring

Whatever way the river flows
I know my love has wings.

So if the sun should disappear
And the wind should never sing,
Come fly away with me, my Clare.
My love has wings.

And if the flower should never bloom,
The bell should never ring,
Come fly away with me, my Clare.
My love has wings.
Come fly away with me, my Clare.
My love has wings.

PADDY: *Taken by this moment, he rises.* If I had the words to say, which I don't, how you should tell Clare of your love, I couldn't come close to yours… there is so much elegance… even eternity, in your words… a love with wings… I can think no greater love…

ALOIS: Just a poem…

PADDY: Alois, I want two promises from you.

ALOIS: No promises, Pata. Except, I will try.

PADDY: Close enough. Promise me you'll tell Clare of your love. Share that poem with her. Once you do that, you'll feel a great heaviness leave your heart, and in its place, hopefully, will be her love for you. Can you do that? Do it for Clare, more than for yourself.

ALOIS: Hmmm. Well, I can agree. I must do that. That, at least. I knew there must be one good reason to bring you here.

PADDY: I'm not finished, Alois.

ALOIS: Oh, I forgot. Pata Paddy is never finished. I should know that.

PADDY: Alois, listen. If Clare doesn't want you… the Capuchins want you.

ALOIS: Pata, I would make, well, you have a Pennsylvania word for it, I believe, lousy… a lousy priest. No, Alois, a priest? I don't think so.

PADDY: You have the fabric, believe me.

ALOIS: I am too much Huli to be a priest.

PADDY: I am striving to become more Huli, Alois. The more Huli I am, the better priest I will be. A priest is not a saint, walking on air, spouting off about Christ and the gospels. Well, maybe part of the time. No. A priest is someone who feels a great love inside, and wants to get that love outside of him, where it might do some good. That IS you, Alois. You have a great love inside you. Why you can make a great priest.

ALOIS: I have a great many loves, yes. But a priest, no. I cannot conceive of it. It is beyond me.

PADDY: Anyway, my heart is at peace, because I have planted this seed in you. Just don't throw it into the river, ok?

ALOIS: If I don't have Clare, I can think of nothing else. Nothing in this world. Even life itself…

PADDY: *A sudden thought.* Alois, you know what my favorite uncle used to do, my Uncle Chuck? He liked to write poems, little poems for my Aunt Pauline. You know what he used to do?

ALOIS: Am I to guess?

PADDY: He'd leave poems in the most unexpected places. Little love poems. For his Pauline to find. Poems that would make her smile. Or touch her heart. She might be doing the wash, and she'd find a poem. I see her laughing in the cellar beside that old wringer washer, checking the pocket of his work pants, and finding a poem. Or she might reach into her dresser drawer for her nightie and find a love poem there.

ALOIS: He was full of love, as you are.

PADDY: Alois. Why don't you leave a poem where Clare will find it? In her pocket. Or the wash room. Or…

ALOIS: Her bilum, I could easily put it there.

PADDY: Yes. Perfect. In her bilum.

ALOIS: She leaves it lying everywhere, so careless. Yes, I'll put my poem in her bilum.

PADDY: But first, you must talk to her, tell her of your love.

ALOIS: Perhaps. Anyway, you are Huli, today. Thanks to SumiSami. Now all you need is a SumiSami bone to wear around your neck along with your tau. Are you willing?

PADDY: A relic. Of SumiSami. Ha. What will my Capuchin brothers say? They will shake their heads.

ALOIS: They will say, that Paddy. He must be Huli now. First, we must go and find your relic. At the bottom of this cliff.

PADDY: Ok, lead the way. And get those wings ready, in case I fall, you rascal. Ha. A relic. Saint SumiSami. Ha.

They exit.

SFX: Drums, descending the rhythm.

Go to black.

Possible intermission.

Act Two
Scene Five

The mission, late afternoon.

SFX: Drum segue.

TOM is seated, reading, intent. CLARE comes in with a small basket of vegetables, goes to the sink. TOM looks over at her, and back to his book. CLARE says nothing, but smiles sweetly. She fusses about. TOM is struggling for the right words.

TOM: Clare, about this morning.

CLARE: This beautiful moning.

TOM: Most beautiful… but perhaps…

CLARE: Ating… about Pata Tom all day. Ating… I make yu hepi.

TOM: It… wasn't right… I'm sorry.

CLARE: Most beautiful… right always… no sorry. No, so hepi.

TOM: Yes… Yes… I don't know…

CLARE: Tink about what you say… SumiSami.

TOM: And?

CLARE: Clare take you there?

TOM: When?

CLARE: Tomorrow? Yu mi.

TOM: Tomorrow. Yes. The Day of Independence. They'll all be celebrating. We won't be missed.

CLARE: Celebrate with Huli sing sing. You know sing sing?

TOM: I know about it. Pata Paddy says it is quite something.

CLARE: Someting, all right… But this In-de-pen-dunce. Mean no thing. Huli no change.

TOM: Look for one good thing.

CLARE: One gud ting. Yes.

TOM: You are my one good thing. Since I've come here. This is the first day I've felt… My one good thing.

CLARE: Pata. You my one gud ting.

TOM wants to take her in his arms, but Clare politely refuses.

CLARE: No here… no gut.

TOM: When, Clare, when…

CLARE: Tomorrow.

TOM: Tomorrow. Don't know if I can wait that long.

CLARE: SumiSami for us maybe, you tink?

TOM: You will take me there?

CLARE: Clare take you.

CLARE cleans vegetables, puts short distance between them.

CLARE: Man and woman go SumiSami, they have love. Mangalim tru.

TOM: I… I just want you, Clare.

CLARE: Have love all time. SumiSami… make them… one… they marry…

TOM: Clare, help me… my one good thing…

CLARE: Shhhh. Tomorrow. SumiSami.

MOSES enters with mail.

MOSES: Mail come. Yu got name on.

TOM: Thank you, Moses. So the rascals didn't get it this time.

MOSES: Moses keep job… maybe?

TOM: What? Oh, yes, of course. We need you, Moses. I was upset this morning. I was angry, do you understand? I must apologize.

MOSES: No understand Pata Tom.

TOM: I said I'm sorry. Surely you understand that?

MOSES: Understand sorry. No understand Pata Tom.

TOM: *Sorting through the mail.* That makes the two of us. Don't understand you either. So much for an apology. You need to understand forgiveness, Moses. It's the Christian way. You can't be a Christian until you learn to forgive. *He finds the letter he's looking for, opens it.*

MOSES: Key to petrol. You want me show you where? You say you want lock and key... so...

TOM: *Annoyed at being interrupted.* Yes. I heard you. On the table. That's fine. Anything else?

MOSES: *Puts key on the table.* Tomorrow sing sing. Moses no wok. No look for Moses tomorrow.

TOM: Sing sing. Yes. Any excuse not to work. Whatever. I really don't care.

Tom reads the letter, likes what it contains.

Off, PADDY and ALOIS approaching, laughing.

TOM stuffs the opened letter into his pocket.

PADDY and ALOIS enter, tired, but still elated. PADDY has a small bone on the same string with his tau, around his neck.

PADDY: We're back. Made it in one piece. Though I'm not so sure about SumiSami.

ALOIS: Pata Paddy is a true Huli now. Look what he brings back with him.

MOSES stands aside, clearly annoyed.

PADDY: A bone. I'll wear it with my tau. It is my relic from Saint SumiSami. Oh, what an adventure, one for the books, for sure.

ALOIS approaches CLARE.

ALOIS: Apinoon, Clare.

CLARE: Apinoon, Alois. So, Pata Paddy like SumiSami?

PADDY: Clare, the most wonderful place. Never seen anything like it. I can understand why lovers go there. A good hike, too. You've been there, Clare?

CLARE: Many times. Go with mama.

PADDY: Teasing. Go with mama? You ought to go with Alois.

ALOIS is surprised. CLARE is annoyed.

CLARE: No. Alois busy look in riva.

PADDY: Tom, you have to see it, utterly amazing. You can see for miles. All across the Waghi Valley. Must be fifty, perhaps a hundred. Nothing compares to it.

TOM: Yes… I'd like to… like to see it. Love to go there.

PADDY: You look down, it's like looking up at the sky… no end to it… there is no bottom. Took us nearly an hour to get to the base of the cliffs, but it was worth it.

ALOIS: However, it took Pata Paddy only ten minutes to find his relic. I believe it is a cassawary bone, but he insists.

PADDY: Oh, no, no, this is SumiSami's bone, and I have other plans for this relic, you wait.

MOSES: *Angry.* Make fun of SumiSami. Not like Pata Paddy.

PADDY: Oh, no, Moses, never. SumiSami is a sacred place. Ples masali, huh? Today… I begin to understand Huli, and why you Moses, are so careful not to let go of it. True. Have always admired that about you.

MOSES: Ahhh, but this bone around neck… You not Huli.

PADDY: I wear it with respect. For everything Huli

TOM: Tell me more about it, Paddy.

PADDY: You have to see it, Tom. A story from the Huli bible... Listen. All the way back, I was thinking about SumiSami, about tomorrow, and the Day of Independence. And the mass we will have... to celebrate. Here are my plans.

They sit, except TOM, who stands off to the side, like Judas.

PADDY: We will celebrate the mass together. And all our people will be there. Alois and Moses, you will paint yourselves as great Huli warriors. We will kill a pig and roast it in the ground. We will share this day and all it means. Moses, he is one of your prophets. Matthew, Mark, Luke and John. And SumiSami. Ha. The story could have come right out of the mouth of Jesus. But we will save that for tomorrow... For now, I'm taking a shower. And then we'll eat dinner. Alois, will you join us?

ALOIS: No, Pata. I will go and rest, and eat later. Perhaps Clare will join me?

CLARE: Busy make dinner, then go sleep. Wok hard all day, Alois.

PADDY: Tom, I'll tell you more about it over dinner, every detail.

TOM: Paddy, I need to share something with you. Do you have a moment?

PADDY: Of course. What is it?

TOM: It's... well, not here... Can we go outside?

PADDY: Of course. Walk with me.

PADDY and TOM exit.

MOSES: So, Alois, we will be Huli warriors tomorrow.

ALOIS: Yes.

MOSES: Do you forget how?

ALOIS: How could I forget? You teach me everything. We will

prepare together, before mass. A Huli mass. Ah, that Pata Paddy…

MOSES: That Pata Paddy. He long long, this independence.

CLARE: Pata Paddy gudman. He see Huli in you, Moses. He love SumiSami. He gudman.

MOSES: Tomorrow, Alois. You come to my hut, you ok? Huli warrior, ok?

ALOIS: Ok, Moses.

MOSES exits.

Alone, now, CLARE stays busy with her food preparation, ALOIS moves closer to her.

ALOIS: Clare…

CLARE: You change mind, hungry Alois?

ALOIS: Water. Just some water. *Pours himself a glass from a pitcher on the table.*

CLARE: You sit and rest. Hard walkabout… SumiSami.

ALOIS: …I love to watch you work.

CLARE: Yes. All men like. Luk luk woman wok. Tsk tsk.

Lights down on ALOIS and CLARE.

Act Two
Scene Six

PADDY and TOM outside the mission.

TOM takes the letter from the pocket of his habit.

TOM: Paddy, I received this letter today.

PADDY: The mail arrived. Good. You seemed anxious it. I knew you were expecting something.

TOM: Yes. Well, it's from Father Paul. I wrote to him about my situation. Requesting… a change. To St. Fidelis Seminary in Madang. I really need to study and teach theology. I believe that's my calling. I didn't want to worry you. That's why I haven't spoken about it before…

PADDY: You speak about it every day, it's written all over you. Still, I was hoping… well… hey, I appreciate you sharing this with me. So what does Fr. Paul say?

TOM: He will seriously consider it.

PADDY: I'd take that as a yes.

TOM: He will find a replacement for me here. I insisted on that. Not to leave you alone here in the jungle.

PADDY: This is good news for you, Tom. So I'm happy for you. You are not to worry.

TOM: Paddy, I will miss you, I truly will. It will be hard to say good-by.

PADDY: A wise man once said, every time we say good-by, it is a preparation for our death. And every time we make a new friend, it is a preparation for heaven. So my prayer for you… is that you make some new friends. I think you need that.

TOM: You have a philosophy even for saying good-by.

PADDY: Helps get me through the day, Tom. We can talk about this over dinner.

TOM: And Paddy… tomorrow. I'm not one for the celebrating. I think I'll take a walk in the jungle, contemplate my decision. Do you mind?

PADDY: If you need that. I guess I understand.

TOM: Thank you…

PADDY exits.

Lights down on TOM holding the letter, come up on the interior of the mission.

ALOIS and CLARE, as before.

SFX: Drums, of course, are the segue.

ALOIS: Clare. Come with me tonight to the river?

CLARE: No tonight. Busy get ready.

ALOIS: I must talk to you, Clare. I have been thinking about you all day.

CLARE: You with Pata all day. Clare nating.

ALOIS: You are all I think about any more, all I ever think about. I must talk to you.

CLARE: Clare here. You tok.

ALOIS: Here?

CLARE goes up to him with a "get it over with" attitude.

CLARE: Clare here.

ALOIS: Very well. Clare…

CLARE: Huh…

ALOIS: Don't you know how I feel about you…?

CLARE: How Clare know? You no say.

ALOIS: Clare… I love you very much… Mangalim yu.

CLARE: *Turns away, hurt.* Ohhhhh.

ALOIS: I do. I love you, Clare…

CLARE: Alois, no…

ALOIS: Why no. I love you, Clare…

CLARE: Can no be…

ALOIS: My love for you is so big, Clare, I cannot hold it in. We can be so happy, Clare. I have big plans. We will leave Tari and live in a better place. I will work hard for you, and I will be faithful to you. I would never let any harm come to you. Our Huli brothers and sisters will bless us. If you will... Clare... look at me... I have a poem... let me say it to you... My love has wings... Then you will understand... listen...

CLARE: *Turns her back, confused, a little sad.* Aloĩs, no...

ALOIS: "The morning has its mist and dew, the sunshine has it's sky, the..."

CLARE: Alois... no... no more... plis...

ALOIS takes her in his arms, but she breaks away.

CLARE: No, Alois, no, no....

ALOIS: Clare, I love you so much. I want to be with you all the time. I decided... at SumiSami... today... that I will marry you.

CLARE: No, no, Alois. Never can be... Clare no love Alois.

ALOIS pulls away.

ALOIS: Never? How can you say never? I will always love you. Be with me, Clare.

ALOIS tries to kiss her, and again, CLARE breaks away.

CLARE: No love Alois. Clare love... other... someone... other...

ALOIS: *Steps away from her.* What?

CLARE: *Kindly.* Clare love another.

ALOIS: Who, Clare? Who can you love?

CLARE: It... Secret. Secret man.

ALOIS: You must tell me. I don't believe you.

CLARE: Clare love... gudman. So nice...

ALOIS: Tell me who. I will fight for you. I will fight like a Huli warrior for you.

CLARE: Must no say. It secret.

ALOIS: You must tell me. Who do you love?

CLARE: Make Huli promise.

ALOIS: Who is it? Clare, tell me…

CLARE: Make Huli promise.

ALOIS: *Angry.* Make promise. Tell me.

CLARE: Clare love… Pata Tom.

ALOIS: …Pata Tom… Pata Tom!

CLARE: …Alois…

ALOIS: Clare, he is a priest. He will never love you.

CLARE: He gudman. Love Pata Tom.

ALOIS: Never. He cannot love you. You must get this out of your head. Pata Tom is a… Pata… Understand? A priest cannot love a woman. Clare… you are so foolish.

CLARE: Pata Tom love Clare. I his one gud ting… Alois, you forgive. I love Pata Tom.

ALOIS: Pata Tom. Pata Tom!

ALOIS runs from the mission.

CLARE: *Calls him, her love tinged with remorse, near tears.* Alois, you forgive! Alois… Alois…

SFX: Drums up softly, sadly.

End of Act Two.

Act Three
Scene One

The mission, next morning.

SFX: The drums wake us.

PADDY and TOM are kneeling side by side, backs to us, in their capuchin habits. They each have the cowl (hood) over their heads. They could be twins. Praying aloud from their breviary, they go back and forth, as is the tradition, answering each other. TOM reads the pidgin slowly, PADDY speaks it fluently. Finishing their prayers, they're at the end of the Our Father.

TOM: Pogivim rong… bilong mipela…

PADDY: Olsem mipela I pogivim ol arapela I mekim rong long mipela.

TOM and PADDY TOGETHER: Na rausim olgeta samting nogut long mipela. Amen.

They get up, PADDY gets coffee for them both. TOM is troubled.

PADDY: Well, you must have been thinking about your decision for a long time.

TOM: Yes, for some time now.

PADDY: Madang is hot, too hot for me. But they say the most beautiful in the South Pacific.

TOM: The ocean, the awesome Pacific, black sand beaches. But of course, there are rascals everywhere in this country.

PADDY: True, but they can't steal the sunset and the sand and that gorgeous sky.

TOM: Wouldn't put it past them.

PADDY: Something troubling you, Tom? Still? You got your wish, you're going to Madang.

TOM: *Caught off guard.* Why do you say that? No… Well, yes, of course… all this business… deserting you. Leaving you this mess.

PADDY: Messy, at times, yes. But not a mess. A mission. A moment in God's eternity. Don't feel sorry for me, Tom. You know I love it. And today, the day of Independence. It will be a new beginning. I'm glad you're not leaving Papua New Guinea. We're holding on to you until this place takes a hold on you.

TOM: Paddy, do you remember, I said today, this morning, I need to spend some time thinking about this. Go off for a while. Take a good hike.

PADDY: Well… yes… But there's a lot to do, not the best day for a hike.

TOM: I want to help. But I need this. You know it always comes together.

PADDY: Somehow, huh? You're right, it does. Go off if you must. We'll pray for your decision. Our mass of celebration is 6 PM, after the sing sing. Tom, it will be glorious. What a day this is.

TOM: Be back this afternoon.

PADDY: Don't get caught in the rain. Could come at any time.

TOM: I like the rain. The sound of it. Drowns everything out. Once I stood outside in it for the longest time. Alois saw me and started laughing. Made me angry. I probably said something to him.

PADDY: Tom, do you ever laugh at yourself? Try it sometime. St. Francis did, that holy fool. Very humbling. He who expects nothing, remember?

TOM: Shall be gloriously surprised.

PADDY: We might get a glorious surprise from Alois.

TOM: What's that?

PADDY: In confidence, now, huh? I have your assurance?

TOM: Of course.

PADDY: We had the greatest chat yesterday at SumiSami. He is so in love with Clare. You could see it in his eyes.

TOM: Clare… huh… She… is a beautiful girl.

PADDY: You've noticed. How could you not. But still so young. Flits from one thing to the next. Delightfully. The way young people should, while they have the chance.

TOM: So you lost your priest.

PADDY: Maybe not. That's wat I'm telling you. I advised him to tell Clare of his love. He was telling me, of all people. I'm not going to marry him. He has to tell Clare. She's the one must know.

TOM: Good advice.

PADDY: But listen, I said, if she turns you down, the Capuchins want you. We'll take your love. Marry the Capuchins, instead. And I put that seed in him.

TOM: And what did he say to that?

PADDY: I think he was flattered. He is in love beyond distraction. But the seed is there. I wanted you to know. I told him he could marry the Capuchins at SumiSami, ha.

TOM: What was it like, SumiSami?

PADDY: I have to take you there. The most gorgeous valley I've ever seen. Alois believes I'm the first white man to put my eyes upon it. Honored.

TOM: Yes, I… I'd like to go there.

PADDY: The jungle wraps you up in its vines, tangles you in its embrace and releases you on this spot and if you weren't in love before, you are surely in love now. I believe lovers seek out places that match their rapture, as painters do, as Gauguin did in Polynesia, as Monet did in Quarles. The church should allow us to marry people at such places.

TOM: Did your magic work on Alois?

PADDY: Not magic. Just a seed planted. You can help, Tom. If he shows the slightest inclination, talk to him... about your own priesthood.

TOM: Wouldn't be much of a salesman at the moment.

PADDY: Who better? You're about to go off and teach theology. We have to... reach him from every angle. Gentle pressure, and much love. We can win him over... if Clare...

TOM: Clare. She's our ticket to his priesthood. Perhaps we should talk to Clare.

PADDY: Oh, not so sure about that.

TOM: Yes. Clare. Do you think she'll be surprised?

PADDY: They're always surprised. Never surprised. One of the many gifts God gave women. Men have been guessing ever since. Usually guessing wrong. But women need that edge. Since men can be so deceiving.

TOM: You think so?

PADDY: Wait until you've heard as many confessions as I have. It's a joke. On themselves. Men never learn.

TOM: Then why do we do this?

PADDY: Because we never give up. We fall, we get up, we fall, we get up, we fall, and one of these days, we can't get up, and it's over.

TOM: I didn't know you to be so fatalistic.

PADDY: Tom, surely you know this. We're headed for oblivion, all of us. But the way there, the way to oblivion, it's a struggle, and it's a delight, hand in hand.

TOM: Oblivion.

CLARE enters with an armload of clean laundry.

CLARE: MORNing, Pata Paddy, Pata Tom. MORNing.

PADDY: MORNing, Clare. Practicing your English?

CLARE: Pata Tom help. Tenkyu tru, Pata Tom. He tisim Inglis.

PADDY: That's good, improve your English, nice.

CLARE: *To TOM.* And I tisim tok pison. Bargain?

TOM: *Embarrassed to take her hand, he starts to leave.* It was just a short lesson. Excuse me. I've some reading to do.

TOM exits.

CLARE: He gudpela, Pata Tom. Helpim me.

PADDY: Well, you're a nice person to help.

CLARE: This best wonderful day.

PADDY: Best wonderful? Can't get much better than that.

CLARE: Hear bird sing. See Pata Paddy smile, see Pata Tom… he helpim Inglis. Clare happy.

PADDY: Clare…

CLARE: *Keeping busy in the kitchen.* Yes…

PADDY: Clare…

CLARE: Clare here.

PADDY: Do you think Alois….

CLARE: Alois, yes…

PADDY: Do you think he would make a good priest?

CLARE: Alois? Pata?

PADDY: Yes, Alois, a priest. What do you think?

CLARE: *Laughs.* Alois… Pata…? Pata Alois…? *Puts a towel in her mouth to stop her laughter.*

PADDY: *Smiling.* Is that your answer?

CLARE: So sorry… Tell yu tru, Alois make good anyting. Pata? Clare go confession Pata Alois? No happen. Why Clare laugh. He learn all Clare tink? No happen. He crazy, Alois. Long long for Clare.

PADDY: Crazy for Clare?

CLARE: One touch, go long long. Alois, a pata? …Pata Paddy, you long long, too. *Laughs.* You crazy, Alois crazy. Maybe all men long long, huh?

PADDY: Yes. Maybe we are. *He goes to the vestments in the corner.* I think… yes… this will be a mass of celebration… white vestments… what do you think, Clare. Shall I wear white?

CLARE: White? Nonono. Red. Clare like red. Red happy, much color. Red make feel good. Red my color, see? *She twirls in her red skirt.*

PADDY: Clare, you are one happy Huli this morning. Happy all the time, of course. But this morning, especially. What makes Clare so happy? That is a great quality, you know.

CLARE: Qual-la-tee. No understand.

PADDY: You have something very special in you, this happy way that you are. It's a great gift… a quality you have, then. Understand?

CLARE: No. Clare just hepi… Have one gud ting.

PADDY: What's that? One what?

CLARE: *Laughs.* You tok tok tok, so much this morning. MORNing. How Clare sound?

PADDY: Good. An improvement. So Pata Tom is helping you?

CLARE: He nice. He helpim Inglis. I help tok pison.

PADDY: News to me… when did this begin?

CLARE: Moning, afta breakfast time. He nice… So, you go SumiSami, Pata Paddy.

PADDY: Oh, Clare, it is wonderful.

CLARE: You go with Alois. I find laughing. Oh, my.

PADDY: Why, what's so funny about that?

CLARE: You and Alois… SumiSami. Ples for love… man, woman go… get marry… love… understand? Love?

PADDY: I think so, Clare. Priests understand, believe me. My parents were in love, I saw that in them every day. My mother was always humming a love song. And I see love all around me. When I marry people, I wear white. A celebration of love.

CLARE: Pata no marry. Why? Yu in love, yu marry. Yu say so. Beautiful, yu say. So. Why no Pata? Helpim Clare understand.

PADDY: I'm married to my priesthood. To my vow, my promise, to give my life to God. That is what I have been called to do. You understand? This is what I must do to serve God, and God only. This is my love. Fully, with everything I have. So I promise… not to marry. A priest cannot have two wives.

CLARE: Pata no marry? No time?

PADDY: Sometimes they do, but they break their promise…

CLARE: Oh, pata sometime marry?

PADDY: It happens… Yes, it does happen…

CLARE: Ohhh.

PADDY: …and then they must leave the priesthood It is forbidden. It is wrong. It is as if… look here…

CLARE sits beside him

PADDY: …if a man is married, and he leaves his wife for another woman, is that right?

CLARE: Bad men do, planti bad men, tell you tru. Man bilong me, he stay… he stay with Clare, Clare make hepi. Clare make hepi all day. Clare make hepi all night. *Wistfully.* …all night.

PADDY: I'm sure. But, just as it is wrong for a man to leave his wife, and break his promise, it is wrong for a priest to leave his priesthood, and break his. Understand?

CLARE: No. But ok… Clare hepi. *She gets up to leave.* And yu go to SumiSami with Alois, I find laughing. *Stops, pauses.* That Alois. What I do with him?

PADDY: Yes, that is the question, what will we do with Alois?

CLARE: No want hurt him. But he crazy, crazy for me. So long long, I worry, my goodness.

PADDY: He told you that?

CLARE: I tell him. No, Alois. Can never be. Clare no love Alois.

PADDY: Are you sure you want to share this with me?

CLARE: You Pata Paddy, tell you anyting… Alois no understand. Tell you tru… no want hurt Alois.

PADDY: Clare, you are young. Love needs time. Give this time. There is no rush.

CLARE: Rush?

PADDY: No hariap, Clare. Isi, go isi. Think about this. You don't want to lose Alois, do you?

CLARE: *Laughing.* Too late, you and Alois go SumiSami, now you and Alois have love. You and Alois. You help Clare, go SumiSami with Alois. Ha. Tenkyu tru, Pata Paddy. Clare hepi now. Tenkyu tru, SumiSami.

CLARE exits.

PADDY sits, thinking he has botched it.

Fade out.

SFX: Drums take us into the hut of MOSES.

Act Three
Scene Two

Fade in on MOSES, squatting on the ground. He is mixing some colors into a paste. He has painted his arms with a red and yellow patina, has started to paint his face yellow. The machete lies at his side.

ALOIS enters.

ALOIS: Time for warpaint, already? Bilas bilong yu.

MOSES: Bilas long pes bilong mi.

ALOIS: Your own warpaint. Bilas bilong yu. For Moses.

MOSES: For Pata Paddy. Day Independence. Celebrate, he say. Have sing sing, so Moses get ready. Mi yu, Alois. Show Huli, how gut is to be Huli.

ALOIS: You keep our past alive, Moses. But I am looking to the future. I struggle with this. *Picks up a mask, holds it over his face.* When I see the past, I wonder where it is taking us.

MOSES: You have taim befo inside you, no need… wonder. This, all this… *Looks around at the paint, the feathers, the headdress nearby.* …this is the stone that holds us in place. The rock that keeps us… Huli.

ALOIS: The cornerstone, eh?

MOSES: No understanding.

ALOIS: The stone upon which all else is built, the stone that holds up all the rest, the rock that makes all else possible.

MOSES: I agree, then. Huli, cornerstone, that is good.

ALOIS: The stone which the builders rejected has become the cornerstone. By the hand of God has this been done, and it is beautiful in our eyes.

MOSES: What is that, bible talk?

ALOIS: One way to put it.

MOSES: Bible talk. Planti problem. Too much bible talk and Huli, poof, fly away like scared bird.

ALOIS: Pata Paddy says if it flies away, it always comes back. That's the way it is with our traditions, our Huli. Why he wants a sing sing along with the mass today. Why he is excited about our Day of Independence. Why he wants to celebrate.

MOSES: Pata Paddy, no understand Pata Paddy.

ALOIS: But he is very simple.

MOSES: You see it too. That is why. He brings his ways, he tisim Christian, and he say everything come together. Look, this yellow paint. What happens I put into blue? Turn into green. Change forever, all time. Now we say green is better. We say yellow still there. But is not. Cannot mix and stay same. You take Pata Paddy to SumiSami yesterday. You mix. You change.

ALOIS: Maybe I make him Huli, huh?

MOSES: Better make Pata Paddy Huli than make Moses Christian, I think.

ALOIS: But you are baptized, it can never be erased.

MOSES: Baptized. Small child. Five of us. We are baptized, mother, pata, children. All in line. One, two, three, four, five. Ha. Try to run away, papa bilongmi grab hand. So I baptize. Remember the water. Afraid it would hurt, pull Huli from heart, start to cry.

ALOIS: Hurt, why would it hurt?

MOSES: Like vaccination. Day before, give long needle in arm, and ohh I cry. I tink, maybe baptism hurt like vaccination.

ALOIS: *Laughs.* Vaccination. I like that. Vaccinated against the devil. If I were I priest, I would use that in a sermon. Maybe I will tell Pata Paddy.

MOSES: You tell pata everything. Tell too much.

ALOIS: Not everything. There is one thing I don't know I can tell him.

MOSES: What is that?

ALOIS: Clare, she says she does not love me. She loves someone else.

MOSES: Clare laik everything. She long long. Go from one to next. Too hepi, sometimes, I tink.

ALOIS: She loves… Pata Tom.

MOSES: Pata Tom? See, she crazy.

ALOIS: When she told me, I was so angry. Wanted to kill him.

MOSES: *Laughs.* Payback in you. See, you Huli. That Pata Tom… He trabelman, no belong, bad for here. Better he go away.

ALOIS: Clare loves him. Could see it in her eyes. I don't know… if I tell Pata Paddy…. He will be so angry. And what could he do?

MOSES: Nating. Can do nating when woman say she in love. Let her go. Tomorrow she love something else. You must wait.

ALOIS: I cannot wait. My life is running and I cannot catch up with it. There is so much to do, so much I want to do, and now this. Clare in love with… a priest.

MOSES: What else she say? She talk about Pata Tom?

ALOIS: No. Just that she loves him, love him tru.

MOSES: Then you go to Pata Tom. Tell him. He the one fixim.

Look him in eyes, say, Clare say she love you. What we do now? Hear what he say. I don't like. No belong here. You go to Pata Tom.

ALOIS: What would I say to him? That Clare is in love with him? He would laugh at me.

MOSES: Tell him… stay away from Clare. Tell him, no touch. Tell him, one touch, yu kilim strong. Ha. I tink, he understand… kilum.

ALOIS: Ahh, Moses, you think the Huli way solves everything. I cannot do that. I make a mistake when I run away from Clare. The anger in me makes me another person. I must talk to Clare.

MOSES: Tok to Clare. Then tok to Pata Tom. Tell him, one touch, yu kilum. Huh, he understand.

MOSES laughs, reaches out and puts a streak of yellow paint on Alois's nose.

ALOIS: Laughing. My nose is Huli, anyhow. *With his finger, begins painting his face yellow.* Ok, Pata Paddy wants Huli, he gets Huli, ok, Moses?

MOSES: Ok.

Lights down, come up on TOM in the jungle.

Act Three
Scene Three

The jungle.

TOM is stooped over, picking at the ground. He wears hiking boots, clothes.

CLARE enters. She has a billum with some fruit in it. CLARE watches him for a moment, smiling.

CLARE: *Whispers.* SumiSami… SumiSami…

TOM: Clare. Have you been standing there?

CLARE: *Softly.* SumiSami.

TOM: *Going to her.* You look beautiful.

TOM embraces her, but she gently resists.

CLARE: Long walk. SumiSami… you ok?

TOM: I'm ready.

CLARE runs off and TOM runs after her.

TOM: Wait, Clare. Wait….

Act Three
Scene Four

The mission.

Lights down, come up on the interior of the mission.

SFX: Radio announcer with details of Independence Day. Some static, as before. It is rather loud. The static drowns out the announcer.

PADDY turns it off.

PADDY: Someday, God will send me a true radio, without a devil in it.

PADDY begins taking tubes of ointment, small bottles of medicine from a box that has arrived and puts them on a shelf, along with others already there. His pharmacy, a bookcase with a few shelves, boxes, tubes of ointment, arranged in his own peculiar filing system.

ALOIS enters. His nose and forehead are painted yellow.

ALOIS: You need some help, Pata?

PADDY: Help is always welcome… ahh, half of a Huli. Is this a new tribe?

ALOIS: Very good. Half of a Huli. That is me.

PADDY: Hand me that other box, please. This is wonderful, what I have been waiting for… for so long. Just arrived. Took nearly seven months. And the rascals didn't get it, thank God for that.

ALOIS: What is it?

PADDY takes another box from the floor, reaches in and pulls out a few tubes of ointment.

PADDY: From my Pharmacist friend in Pittsburgh, Pennsylvania. For skin disease, Oxymiacin. And this, Ceprador, for the eyes, especially red eye. So contagious. Do you remember last year?

ALOIS: Yes, I remember. *Takes out a small box.* What is this?

PADDY: Epsom salts. So wonderful for so many things. Drink it with water to help your stomach or intestines. Soak a cloth with it and help heal a wound.

ALOIS: For both inside and out. How does one know?

PADDY: One knows. True. My mother used it all the time. Seven of us, every day, it seemed. Very effective. And here, look, what we have been missing for months.

ALOIS: Yes, for malaria, correct?

PADDY: Yes, just one pill a day, and in two weeks, the malaria is gone. We must never lose another child to malaria, Alois. Never. Not one more.

ALOIS: When the news gets out, the line will be long.

PADDY: Let it be long. The need is great.

ALOIS: Do you have anything for… a sick heart?

PADDY: Ohhhh. Well, now. Let me see. Here it is. *Picks up a tube.* Patience. That is one cure. Here. *Picks up another.* Always helps, a cure for many things… And this one. Cures absolutely everything. *Holds up a tube.*

ALOIS: Everything? Must be very special. And very expensive.

PADDY: Yes, all of that. Can be very, very expensive. Can take all you have, also can take years, but does cure everything, and guaranteed to make you happy.

ALOIS: *Reaches for it but PADDY pulls it away.* Oh I will buy it. Please.

PADDY: It cannot be bought. It can only be given. That is why it takes so much from you. Why it can take so much time. Why it is so expensive. And why it is so effective.

ALOIS: Tell me, so I can give it, then, and get better.

PADDY: It doesn't come in a tube. It comes from here. *He touches his heart.*

ALOIS: Is it love, then?

PADDY: Love is one ingredient. Understanding, another. Faith, also. Mix carefully with wisdom, just enough. Begin with small doses, increase as needed, give as often as possible.

ALOIS: I think I know… it is too expensive for me.

PADDY: If you already know what it is, then you already have it, enough to heal your heart.

ALOIS: Is it… forgiveness?

PADDY: Do you remember that great poem of St. Francis, The Canticle of the Sun?

ALOIS: You required every one of your students to recite it. How could I forget?

PADDY: "Praise be you, Lord, for all who give pardon through your love…

ALOIS: "And bear infirmity and tribulation…"

PADDY: "Blessed are those who endure in peace…"

ALOIS: "For by you they will be…"

PADDY: …they will be, what?

ALOIS: "Crowned."

PADDY: Yes! Crowned. The highest honor. Anyone can be saved, please Lord, I'm sorry, and the Lord saves you. You're forgiven. But to forgive someone else, that's the pinnacle. You hit the jackpot. That's it. The very jackpot, and you will not just be saved, you'll be crowned, like a king. That's what forgiveness does for you, Alois.

ALOIS: …so difficult…

PADDY: God knows it is difficult, and that's why the reward is like no other.

ALOIS: I don't know…

PADDY: You have it, you see? Now you must learn to give it away. In return, you will receive more gifts, more love, more patience, more faith, more wisdom, more of everything, until you are nearly overwhelmed with the joy of forgiveness. But first… you must begin…

ALOIS: I don't know if I can forgive her. Yesterday, yes. Today, I don't know.

PADDY: What happened to change your mind?

ALOIS: I cannot talk about it.

PADDY: Try me.

ALOIS: Clare is… wild, with her love. She scatters it like the wind. Lets it land where it falls. And will let it blow away with the wind again, I'm sure. I don't understand her. She doesn't stop and think.

PADDY: It can be a strong wind that comes from nowhere and takes us to another place. But the Irish have a saying.

ALOIS: More Irish philosophy.

PADDY: The salmon love the home shore best.

ALOIS: We all come back, eh?

PADDY: To where you belong, to the place where your heart is, to the people you love, all of us. Clare is no different.

ALOIS: I'm afraid that this wind will hurt Clare, hurt her terribly. Before she returns.

PADDY: Returns from where?

ALOIS can't find the words.

PADDY: So, you told Clare of your love, but it didn't go as you wanted.

ALOIS shakes his head no.

PADDY: I'm responsible… I advised you… to share your beautiful poem… I'm sorry, Alois.

ALOIS: No, you were right. Otherwise, how else would I know… she says she is in love… with another.

PADDY: No. True?

ALOIS: She laughed at me… at my poem… would not let me finish, would not listen.

PADDY: Who could she possibly be in love with, no one is worthy of her but you. This will not last. Can you tell me who? I am at a loss. I cannot imagine.

ALOIS: You cannot imagine. I cannot believe. Clare cannot help herself. And I cannot say.

PADDY: Cannot or will not?

ALOIS: I don't know.

PADDY: Sometimes, you think a person is testing your love, but they're really testing their own love, so they do things that are so… unexpected.

ALOIS: And stupid.

PADDY: And crazy.

ALOIS: Hurtful.

PADDY: Mean.

ALOIS: Wretched.

PADDY: Despicable.

ALOIS: Stupid.

PADDY: Back where we started. Who does she love? Who has the wind blown into her life?

ALOIS: *Softly.* Pata Tom.

PADDY: *Can't believe he heard him correctly.* Who?

ALOIS: She says she is in love… with Pata Tom.

> *ALOIS has his back to PADDY, who goes to him, hesitates, turns away, searching for the right words.*

PADDY: Alois, this is not love. This is… infatuation, fantasy, imagination… but not love. It is too sudden, too unexpected, too… *Almost loses it for a moment.* Pata Tom! I don't believe it!

ALOIS: Yes, her one good thing, she calls him.

PADDY: I will talk to him. He is our solution. He will tell her how impossible this is, and this strange, ill wind will blow away, and Clare will learn.

ALOIS: My fear is… what… if he loves Clare?

PADDY: Never. He is a priest. It would be unforgivable.

ALOIS: Pata Paddy, here. *He hands PADDY a tube.* ...some of your medicine.

ALOIS exits.

PADDY: *Calling after him.* I will talk to him, Alois! This will stop! I will end it! I promise! *Alone, now.* Ok, God, now what am I supposed to do? Huh? Need some help on this one. I do. God, help me... Tom, what, what are you thinking!

Lights down, then up on jungle.

Act Three
Scene Five

The jungle.

CLARE runs in, TOM is in pursuit, but out of breath. CLARE kneels down, flushed, but not breathing as hard as TOM is, who follows a moment later. He lays down on his back, catching his breath.

TOM: Why are we running? This is supposed to be a nice walk. Do you want me to catch you? *He reaches out for her, but she teasingly moves away, laughs.* You can't run from me.

CLARE: No run from you, run SumiSami. Wait. You will see. Place for love. So wonderful.

TOM: Clare, let's rest here. Perhaps another day. We will be missed. It's longer than I thought. We should go back.

CLARE: Pata Tom, yu promise.

TOM: *Takes her hand, gently.* Another time. Let's just... sit here and talk. I... need to know you. You are... a mystery to me. So mysterious. So beautiful.

CLARE: Mys-ter-ry. I mys-ter-ry. That nice?

TOM: *Gets closer.* Yes, very nice. Very, very nice. I must solve this… mys-ter-ry… Yes… *And closer.*

CLARE: Listen… Shhhh…

TOM: *Alarmed.* Wha… Is someone coming?

CLARE: Shhhh.

TOM: What?

CLARE: *Softly.* SumiSami… SumiSami… *Laughing, she gets up and runs. Tom gets up and runs after her, laughing also.*

Act Three
Scenes Six, Seven, and Eight

ALOIS, by himself, painting himself, praying.

PADDY in the mission, praying.

CLARE and TOM in the jungle. The love scene.

Note: This scene is sensuous, but not erotic. It must have a touch of elegance.

These three scenes are orchestrated to blend, one to the next, interspersing dialogue, so they are separate, yet together.

SFX: Drums, of course. But also rain and lightning help take us to each of the scenes. The sound of the rain becomes part of the music and helps convey the passion.

ALOIS is finishing painting his face yellow. He has other Huli ornamental garb beside him, prays as he puts it on, and looks like a warrior.

ALOIS: *Praying.* God be my Huli spirit. God be my Huli heart. God be my ancestors. God be my love of my people. God be my yellow mud. God be my Huli blood. God be… be my… my payback!

CLARE and TOM in the jungle. They run in and stop. They have wet hair, shirt, and blouse. The wet may surround her breasts, or not, in good taste. They are very close.

CLARE: Under tree, Pata. Rain come like mountain falling, wait here…

TOM: I love the rain.

CLARE: Rain make nice. Rain make growim. Rain make kau kau. Rain make wet. Ha. *She pulls playfully at her wet blouse.*

TOM: I love only one thing more than the rain.

CLARE: One ting more, only?

TOM: Yes. I love Clare… in the rain.

CLARE: Clare in rain now.

TOM: Yes. Clare in rain now.

He begins to put his hands on her.

CLARE: Yu love Clare in rain.

TOM: Clare love me?

CLARE: Ohhh. Clare love Pata Tom.

He tries to unbutton her blouse, but she stops him

TOM: Clare, love me now. Love me in the rain.

She tries to push him away, but is confused, uncertain.

CLARE: SumiSami. Go SumiSami. Make love there. For marry.

TOM: Here, Clare, here is our love… our maliraim…

CLARE: Oh, maliraim, yes…

TOM: You are so beautiful. You make me so happy. I am your one good thing.

He takes her billum and drops it to the ground.

CLARE: Oh, my one gud ting.

TOM: Make me happy, Clare. Make Pata Tom happy.

CLARE: No here, no here.

TOM: Here, Clare, here. Make Pata Tom happy.

CLARE: Oh, I want… make you hepi. Make you so hepi.

They kiss passionately, kneel together on the ground.

CLARE: Isi… isi… Ohhhh…

SFX: *The rain intensifies as lights go down on them.*

Lights up on PADDY in the mission, talking half to himself, half to his God.

PADDY: God, I need an answer. All right, no answer, just a suggestion. Am I wrong to think the worst? He is a good man. Correction. He is an unhappy good man. Confused. So easy to make a mistake… Where is Clare? She should be here helping me. She never leaves without telling me…

Lights down on PADDY, the stage is almost dark for a moment.

CLARE: isi… isi…

TOM: My one good thing… my one good thing…

CLARE: *Softly.* Ohhhh…

Lights on ALOIS, a Huli warrior, now, with a few finishing touches. After he begins speaking, the rain has stopped.

ALOIS: God be my breath. God be my beating heart. God be my love for Clare. God be my wisdom. God be my passion. God be my forgive… God forgive me, I cannot say forgiveness. God give me forgiveness. I cannot say it.

Lights up on PADDY, blend this scene with ALOIS.

PADDY: Help my love to be humble, Lord. Make me nothing. Make me your servant. Put my people so far above me. Help Tom understand your humble love. Help him know what is right. And where is Clare, where is she? Where is that girl?

While PADDY is praying, lights up on CLARE and TOM as they rise up, silent, after their love making. TOM has conflicting feelings, elation but also remorse. CLARE is quiet, smiling, happy. His back is turned as he buttons his shirt. She is sideways as she modestly straightens her blouse, and looks at him lovingly.

ALOIS: God be my love for Clare. God be our life together. God be her love for me, for me only. Oh, God be that, be her love for me. God be her touch. Her body against mine. God be her loving me forever. God be my forgive... Oh, God help me say it. I cannot. God be my strength.

Lights down on ALOIS and PADDY.

TOM: Oh, oh, it was so wonderful, Clare. Oh, I don't... Oh, God, what have I done... Oh, thank you Clare, thank you.

TOM turns to her, CLARE puts her arms around him. He is confused, just half caresses her, takes a step away.

CLARE: So nice, my one gud ting. Yu love... gud. Clare so hepi. Go SumiSami, go now.

TOM: Oh, Clare... no, not to SumiSami. We must get back. We must think about this. I am confused. You must help me.

CLARE: Oh, I help Pata Tom. We go SumiSami. We marry. We love all time. I make hepi all time. Yu husband, I wife. Love yu so much. Now we love all time. SumiSami, Pata Tom, come.

She takes his hand, pulls him to her, kisses him, gently pulls him to walk with her, but he pulls away.

TOM: No, Clare. No. Not today. Maybe... another day. Clare, this must be our secret. You know secret? No one must know. Only Clare. Must tell no one. Say to no one. Promise.

CLARE: Pata Tom love Clare. Clare now wife. Clare love Pata Tom. Yu love Clare.

TOM: It's not that easy. Not that simple. I am a priest. I can never marry. We are not husband and wife. We made love. Yes. But, no marry…

CLARE: Make love for all time. Huli way. Yu Huli, now. So nice, our love, huh? So nice, my one gud ting.

TOM: Oh, yes, yes, my one good thing, it was… so wonderful.

CLARE: So, make love all time. Come. SumiSami…

TOM: No, Clare, we can never marry. I am a priest. We must ask God to forgive us. Oh, what have I done.

CLARE: Never marry. No understand. You love Clare. You put love into Clare. Now there all time. Clare first time. Yu first time, yu say. Marry, now.

TOM: No. Never. I never said I would marry you. Clare, it cannot be. We can have love, without marry. You understand. Without marry.

CLARE: No understand. No marry? Yu no love Clare?

TOM: I want you. I want you again. And again and again. Let us go back. Must not say anything. Nothing. Secret, please? Please, Clare?

CLARE: *Confused, angry.* No. SumiSami, yu say. Say yu love. Now I belong yu. No belong no other. *Then, sweetly.* We marry, now. Come, please, Pata Tom, SumiSami. Be ok. Understand ok?

TOM: Clare. Look at me. We can never marry. Never. Now let us go back. I have to think about this. What we will do… We must be silent. Must be our secret.

CLARE: No marry Clare?

TOM: Our secret, Clare. Just miyu. Secret. Shhhhh.

CLARE: No marry clare?

TOM: Just miyu... secret... Shhhhh. Must be secret love...

CLARE: You no tru? Yu no stretpela man? Pata Tom...? Yu no save tok tru?

TOM: Clare, we will have this secret... special secret. Ok? We'll make love again. Say yes, Clare. Tomorrow... yes, tomorrow...

CLARE: Oh, Pata Tom...

TOM: Let's go back. Must be secret. Have secret love...

CLARE: No marry Clare? No SumiSami? Ohhhhhhh.

CLARE runs off.

TOM starts to follow, stops, calls after her.

TOM: Clare, don't run away. I do love you. Oh, Clare. Oh... Oh, God...

Lights down, come up on ALOIS, now a complete Huli warrior. He is regal, proud, another person. He picks up his machete, which is also painted. Feels its sharp edge, puts it in its halter on his waist.

ALOIS: God be my Huli. God be my strength. God be my... payback!

MOSES enters, also now a Huli warrior. They could be twins, are so alike —yellow faces, headgear, conch throat shields, ornaments, leather thongs, painted machetes.

MOSES: Mitupela, Huli brata.

ALOIS turns and clasps MOSES'S arm.

ALOIS: Moses brata mitupela.

MOSES: You see, we are a looking glass. We are one. Ancestors know this. What make us same, also make us Huli. You understand, Alois? *Points to his heart.* Huli way best... always here… can never take away. Pata Paddy want sing sing. Day of Independence. He no understand, can never take away Huli. Some things change. Huli never change.

ALOIS: I will help Pata understand. And I will help you understand Pata Paddy. Today is important day for Huli, Moses, you will see that. Our Independence means that now, more than ever, we must preserve, must keep Huli ways as our treasure. Our ancestors are smiling, Moses, smiling on you, on me, smiling on Pata Paddy.

MOSES: We see things the same. We see them not the same.

ALOIS: Today, let us make this a day for Huli, ok?

MOSES: Ok. For Huli. *Clasps his arm again.* Alois, I look for Clare, can no find. Get ready for sing sing, she should put on yellow mud, grandmother kina shell. Huli dress. For sing sing. Someone say… She go with Pata Tom… into jungle… have bilum with prut, banana. Long walk. I think… maybe… SumiSami.

ALOIS: NO. No. It cannot be. Clare!

MOSES: Clare no understand. SumiSami not for Pata Tom. I don't like.

ALOIS: Clare. Oh, Clare. Now what do I do? Moses, are you sure? Not SumiSami…

MOSES: I don't know. I think… can be.

ALOIS: It is not right. Pata Tom and Clare. My love has wings, my Clare. What are you thinking, SumiSami. No!

MOSES: Must tell Pata Tom, one touch, yu givem gudwan! Yu killim! One touch, Huli way. Then he understand. You want Moses go? Moses go and find.

MOSES starts to exit.

ALOIS: *Stopping him.* No, Moses. I must go. It is my love. My Clare.

I will tell him. One touch, I kilim.

ALOIS runs off, MOSES looks after him, smiles at his success.

MOSES: Tell him, one touch, you killim…

Go to black.

Act Three
Scene Nine

The mission.

Lights up on PADDY, the white vestments and chasubles laid across the kneeler. He sits, absorbed, editing his homily.

After a moment, TOM enters. PADDY looks, says nothing. TOM takes a towel, begins drying off, changing his shirt.

PADDY: You're back.

TOM: Yes.

PADDY: The rain…

TOM: Yes. Caught in the rain. Again.

PADDY: You like the rain.

TOM: Yes.

PADDY: I… I can't find Clare. Was she with you?

TOM: *Hesitates.* She wanted to, I told her no. She went with me a short distance. She became upset and ran off.

PADDY: *Relieved.* I thought…

TOM: You thought what?

PADDY: It would not be good if she went with you. You did the right thing.

TOM: Why would she go with me?

PADDY: You just said she did.

TOM: A foolish girl. Says foolish things. Imagines all sorts of things. I told her I needed to be alone. So she ran off. She was not happy about that... but I insisted...

PADDY: Poor Clare. She needs to understand. She will grow up soon. Well... Good Tom, good... yes... Today's Mass, what do you think? Do you want to have some remarks?

TOM: This is your day, Paddy. Your people will want to hear what you have to say, not me.

PADDY: Don't sell yourself short, Tom.

TOM: Your people are expecting it.

PADDY: So appropriate that today's gospel is about the loaves and fishes. I've fashioned a thought around that famous little miracle.

TOM: You will shape it around the right message, as you always do.

PADDY: It's for them. Must always look at it from their point of view. Always.

TOM: We have some time yet, I need to... reflect. Excuse me, Paddy.

PADDY: Of course. The sing sing will begin shortly. And then the Mass. And we will have a feast after Mass. They have killed three pigs for this. Imagine that. I've never known them to kill three pigs. But this is a great day, surely.

TOM is silent. PADDY watches him go to the kneeler, wondering, picks up his homily, studies it. Fade out.

Act Three
Scene Ten

The jungle.

ALOIS stops, looks down, sees the billum, picks it up, holds it to him, looks inside, takes out his poem.

ALOIS: Oh, Clare, my love has wings.

Runs off in the direction of SumiSami.

ALOIS: Clare… Clare…

Act Three
Scene Eleven

The jungle.

As ALOIS exits stage right, CLARE enters stage left, distraught. She falls, crawls the last few feet, rests on her hands and knees.

CLARE: Pata Tom belong mipela. Love Pata Tom tru. SumiSami make ok. SumiSami… helpen mipela… SumiSami… *With some difficulty, she hurries off.* SumiSami…

Act Three
Scenes Twelve, Thirteen, and Fourteen

The mission, the jungle, blended.

Orchestrated to blend together, CLARE hurrying to SumiSami, ALOIS trying to find her, PADDY pacing in the mission, reading his sermon, TOM kneeling in prayer.

ALOIS: Clare! …Clare!

CLARE arrives at SumiSumi. She stands regally, facing the wind, facing a nothingness.

Note: *Perhaps the roof of the mission doubles as the edge of the cliff.*

SFX: *Drums build to a climax.*

CLARE: SumiSami, I here. Take Clare to new love. Clare love bilong no one… SumiSami yu makem bilong Clare. Make fly away. Love fly away. Love have wings. Bilong SumiSami. Take Clare… fly away. Take love in wind… Belong SumiSami… Bilong yu. *CLARE takes a step forward, inches from the edge.* Bilong yu, SumiSami.

A final step, and CLARE leaps, arms out stretched, like a bird, and disappears into the darkness as we go to black.

Lights up on ALOIS, in the jungle, caressing the billum.

ALOIS: *Calling.* Clare! …Clare! …My Clare!

Lights down as he runs off, then up on the mission.

SFX: *Off, the natives singing, music of celebration.*

PADDY: Tom, the sing sing is beginning. We must join them.

TOM: *Still at the kneeler.* In a moment.

PADDY: Please, Tom, now. This is not a time for prayer. It is a time for our people. They expect us. We must join the celebration. Come on.

TOM: Yes, of course. Paddy…

PADDY: Yes, what?

TOM: Will you have some time later? I need to talk.

PADDY: Of course, later. Now we need to join our people. Loosen up, Tom. This is a great moment. A time for laughter… singing… dancing… what a day this is…

They exit.

Act Three
Scene Fifteen

The sing sing at the mission, ALOIS in the jungle.

SFX: Music, singing, drums, accentuated a flute, guitar.

The theater is filled with visuals of a sing sing, orchestrated with the music. Full color, as opposed to the black and white visuals as we entered. The entire theater is alive with the sing sing. There could be several screens, backdrops, scrims. We get glimpses of PADDY dancing by himself, MOSES dancing as a Huli warrior, TOM standing, watching.

ALOIS is still searching for CLARE. As all this reaches a climax, the stage becomes dark, the sing sing fades and stops. Go to black.

Act Three
Scene Sixteen

The mission, the Mass.

Lights up on PADDY and TOM in white vestments. An imagined altar is facing us. TOM sits on the right. PADDY is reading the last words of the gospel.

PADDY: *Reading the end of the gospel…* And so the people went away in wonder at what they had seen, and spread the word throughout Galilee... This is the word of the Lord. *Kisses the bible, closes it, makes the sign of the cross.*

Long nem bilong papa, na bilong young pela boy, na bilong Holi Spirit, amen. My beloved people. Yesterday, you gave me a gift. Yu givim long presen mipela. And today I givim yu long presen.

Shows the pendant around his neck.

I have here... around my neck, something that is sacred to me. It is a small bone. A relic of... SumiSami. True. Yesterday I went there and learned this wonderful story.

I will wear this at all times to remind me of my obligation — to never forget the Huli ways. So this is your gift to me. Tenkyu tru...

Now. My gift to you, is this... Today, I have become a citizen of Papua New Guinea. Yes. I am proud, oh, so proud, now, to be Papuan. To be one of you. To be Huli. I do this because this is where I want to spend the rest of my life. I must tell you... Pata Paddy... hepiman.

In the gutnius today, our first day of freedom. Yours and mine. It is the story of the loaves and fishes. Why did Jesus take those five loaves and two fishes and feed five thousand?

What was He telling us? ...Ung pengi, huh? The main point?

It is this. Sometimes, we think that we are nating. Our lives do not matter. Hidden away in the jungle and no one cares. We are nating, huh, nating. We hear what goes on in the big cities. Such important people. They make the laws. The big machines, the bush plane that flies so high. Me? I am nating. Oh, too bad for me... No. No. What Jesus tells us is this... He makes something wonderful... out of nothing.

Yes. We were nating. And now, we are something wonderful. And we can live each day knowing that each of us is a mirikel...

look around, luk luk, go ahead, yes, look at the miracle beside you, so many miracles. It is something to celebrate, each of us — a miracle.

ALOIS enters, slowly, with the body of CLARE in his arms. Her face, her blouse are bloodied. He is unseen at first by the others. He pauses and takes a few more steps.

PADDY: Today, our first day of independence, remember this… when it comes time to raise our voice, to vote for a new government, to be independent… to be Huli, yes, to be Huli… we are important, we are this country, we are the Lord's miracle. And this we must never, never… forget…

ALOIS takes a few more steps in. TOM sees them first, then MOSES. Then PADDY. They are stunned.

ALOIS kneels and lays her bloodied body before them. PADDY takes a step forward and falls to his knees, as TOM steps backwards. MOSES looks on with anger. Their world has stopped.

SFX: Drums. Solemn. A dirge.

Go to black.

Act Three
Scene Seventeen

The mission, later that evening.

PADDY and TOM in their Capuchin habits. PADDY is reading his breviary, but keeps looking off, distracted.

TOM is sorting through a few books, packing them in a box.

SFX: Drums. A dirge.

TOM: *Annoyed.* Can't they stop those blasted drums, they're driving me insane. They haven't stopped.

PADDY: The Huli are mourning. For a great loss. In Ireland, the women keen. They wail and cry. The drums are crying, crying for a beautiful girl who gave her life. Oh, Alois, that dear boy. He ran to the river. I couldn't find him.

TOM: …I hope she can have a Christian burial? The church says that suicide…

PADDY: *A little short with him.* I know what the church says. She could have slipped and fallen, huh? Who was there? No one. Were you there?

TOM: Why would you say such a thing? Why would you even ask that?

PADDY: Just a question.

TOM: If I were there she'd still be alive.

PADDY: Was she in love with you, Tom?

TOM: Who told you that, in love with me? Absurd.

PADDY: Clare told Alois… that she did not love him… she loved another… and that other… was you… Pata Tom.

TOM: A foolish girl. She loved everything.

PADDY: Did you love her? She was delightful. She would be easy to love.

TOM: *Angry.* I'm a priest. What are you saying? Of course, I saw her beauty. Any man would. But…

PADDY: But…

TOM: But that doesn't automatically mean…

PADDY: Automatically? Was it that easy, your infatuation with her?

TOM: Oh, God, Paddy, what have I done?

PADDY: What have you done?

TOM: Nothing. I've done nothing.

PADDY: Then why are you so upset?

TOM: Clare is dead. That beautiful girl is dead. Perhaps I could have prevented it. I could have stopped it. If I had run after her. She ran away from me. I called for her to come back. But she ran. How was I to know? She was angry. She was saying things to me. She wanted to go to SumiSami, now we marry, she says, I wife, she says, I said it cannot be, she said love forever, I said I am a priest, she didn't understand. Paddy, I tried to make her understand, I did, I tried…

PADDY: Blinded by her love?

TOM: Yes, yes, she was blinded by her love.

PADDY: Not her, Tom. You.

TOM: Me?

PADDY: Yes. You still are, aren't you?

TOM: She was so beautiful, so tender, so good, so loving, so warm, I am still blinded, oh, God forgive me, Paddy, what am I to do, what will happen to me? Can God ever forgive me? I meant her no harm. I could not help myself. It just… happened.

PADDY: You take a long walk in the rain forest with a beautiful girl, alone, with one thing on your mind, and it just… happened… I don't think so.

TOM: Yesterday, she… she kissed me…

PADDY: Yesterday, you allowed her to kiss you. You kissed her, as well, huh? Am I right? So today you walk into the jungle and make love to her. Then she runs away when you tell her you can't marry her, you are a priest. Tom, you are more foolish than Clare ever was. You didn't think of her at all. There was only one thing on your mind.

TOM: I meant her no harm.

PADDY picks up a sock or shirt from the floor.

PADDY: *Nearly in tears.* Dotipela, yu dotipela, pata, she would say, yu sluppy, my goodness… Oh, Clare, my sweet Clare, my boskuk…

TOM doesn't know how to console PADDY. He puts a hand on PADDY's shoulder, but PADDY moves away from him.

TOM: Paddy… Paddy… what will become of me?

PADDY: I don't know. My advice is that you tell the Capuchin Provincal and take the consequences. You may be sent home. You may not. I cannot say.

TOM: Will you say anything?

PADDY: …No. I'm not going to say anything… unless I'm asked. If I'm asked, I must tell the truth. You know me, I hide nothing.

TOM: Why would they ask?

PADDY: You were last with her. Don't you think someone will ask? There will be some sort of civil investigation, in their own inadequate, incompetent way. The Capuchin Provincal is another matter. I know him well. He will ask.

TOM: There's no reason for him to ask. A young girl died, took her own life, there's no connection.

PADDY: You forget, there is a connection, isn't there? And so he will inquire. You and I are not the only ones talking about this. In their small huts, I hear a hundred Huli people whispering. You cannot hide from your foolishness. You can only acknowledge it. But your pride prevents you.

TOM: Who gave you this power to see into someone's soul?

PADDY: It's not a power. It's common sense.

TOM: What am I to do?

PADDY: You are leaving anyhow, for Madang. If that weren't so, I would ask you to leave. It is too complicated for you here, after this. Too dangerous.

TOM: I am worried about the payback. Perhaps she did it for payback. You know how the Huli are. So… evil with it. I despise them for it.

PADDY: Still worried about yourself, Tom? Unless you change, the payback will always be with you, wherever you go. I worry about Alois. About the confidence in our people for their priests.

TOM: Will you hear my confession, Paddy?

PADDY: I was afraid you'd ask.

TOM: Please, Paddy. I need to lift this weight. Surely you can't refuse.

PADDY: If contrition is in your heart, yes. However, if you want to go to confession to seal this secret of yours, then no. Do not use this precious sacrament to hide your foolishness. I tell you in advance, that my penance for you will be… You must come forward with this to the Provincal, and then the two of you will decide what happens next. He will keep it in confidence. As I will in the seal of confession. Can you agree?

TOM: Why must he know? Why can't we keep this between us?

PADDY: Between us and God, you mean. I think, God would want you to do the right thing.

TOM: I don't know what the right thing is any more. I need to confess. Please, Paddy.

PADDY: That will be your penance. To tell the Provincal.

TOM: As you say.

PADDY puts on his stole, pulls up a chair next to the kneeler. TOM kneels.

The light begins to flicker, as in the beginning of Act I.

PADDY: We may be doing this in the dark. That generator is not dependable. I do believe it's getting worse. Have to talk to Moses. He fixim.

TOM kneels with his head down, facing PADDY, who sits, facing sideways. He bows his head in his hands after making the sign of the cross.

PADDY: Whenever you're ready, Tom.

TOM: Bless me father, for I have sinned… It's my pride, Paddy, it's my sin of pride that plagues me, I cannot control it. I just cannot. I try, but it conquers me.

PADDY: Go on.

The lights flicker more, become like strobes, so that the scene takes on an eerie quality.

TOM: … I am conflicted. My pride leads me into temptation, and this time, I was not prepared for the consequences. I tell you, Paddy, it's my pride that is the problem, I know it.

A Huli warrior appears opposite them, fully dressed in Huli paint, feathers, kina shell. You cannot say who it is.

PADDY: Yes, Tom, I know. Take your time. Go on. I'm listening.

TOM: It began innocently enough. She was very sweet to me, very kind.

PADDY: Yes, she was a kind person, so sweet.

TOM: Her touch, Paddy, it put a thrill in me I had never felt in my life, it captivated me, consumed me… I knew it was wrong, but I questioned how wrong it really was. What could be wrong with it. It's the way God made us.

PADDY: Go on.

The Huli warrior slowly takes his machete from its sheath. The lights flicker even more.

TOM: I led her on. Asked her to take me to SumiSami, hoping that would provide a chance... to go further with her...

PADDY: This plan itself was sinful, you understand that, Tom?

TOM: Yes. I do. Now I do. I did then, too. But I didn't care. I just wanted her, in the worst way. I was caught up in the... I was like a child. We were running, laughing... Oh, her laugh... her wonderful laugh...

The warrior takes a few steps towards them, slowly bringing his machete high in the air. He is almost within striking distance.

PADDY: Don't make this more difficult for yourself than you need to, Tom.

TOM: I want you to understand how it was, how it happened, how wonderful it was. It took control of me. And then the rain. It seemed to wash all the sinfulness away, wash away all the doubt, seemed to make it... clean... pure. She was so beautiful, the wetness of her, I needed to feel it, to have it close to me, so I...

The warrior creeps a few steps closer.

SFX: Drums sneak in, ominous.

PADDY: God will help you with this, you must give yourself to God and his forgiveness.

TOM: She was pleading for me to wait, to wait for SumiSami, but I couldn't. My heart was pounding. I was so aroused. Paddy, I... I...

The warrior runs through the strobe, with a heightened stop action effect, machete raised high.

Neither PADDY or TOM look up until perhaps the last instant. The machete comes down as the scene goes completely dark.

WARRIOR: Arrraaagggghhhh!

SFX: A slashing sound, a head falls to the floor.

The lights flicker again, as the head rolls a short distance, followed by a soft light, which dims quickly to black.

SFX: Drums segue from tragedy to mourning to quiet.

Act Three
Scene Eighteen

The mission, a week later. Morning.

A Capuchin is kneeling in prayer with his back to us. We don't know who it is, yet.

Alois enters, watches the Capuchin praying for a moment.

ALOIS: You asked that I stop and see you.

The Capuchin slowly gets up, his back to us.

ALOIS: I don't have much time.

TOM turns and faces him.

TOM: You're really leaving, then?

ALOIS: I have to be in Hagen by one o'clock for my flight to Port Moresby.

TOM: Alois…

ALOIS: The jeep is waiting.

TOM: What can I do to convince you to stay?

ALOIS: Nothing.

TOM cannot hide his fear, the anguish that consumes him.

ALOIS is stoic. He controls his anger. His love for PADDY and CLARE rises above it.

TOM: I need you here, Alois. You... you could be my assistant. Yes. Think about that. You would be... in charge of the catechists. Yes. In preparation for the seminary. Paddy said there was a priest in you.

ALOIS: He could see inside people, no? ...I must be going.

He starts to leave, stops each time TOM speaks.

TOM: Why would he do such a thing? What kind of hatred inside Moses would make him take away the best thing that ever happened to his people, why?

ALOIS: If I told you, you would still not understand.

TOM: Where is he now?

ALOIS: In the bush, of course.

TOM: The authorities will find him. They must. Justice will be done.

ALOIS: If they find him, they will do nothing. The police are Huli, also. They will not arrest one of their own. Besides, Moses is respected, his reason will be accepted.

TOM: What reason could there possibly be?

ALOIS: Moses believes that Pata Paddy brought all the changes, all the ways not Huli, all the acceptance of his people, all the things Moses is against. He also brought you. But killing you would not be enough. Pata Tom, you are nating, nating... Moses believes... You are no stretpella man, you are tusait, you are nating... Moses says... You will go away someday, anyhow. Pata Paddy, never... and then, on our day of independence, Pata Paddy gives up his American citizenship and becomes Papuan... I am Huli now, he says, heh, he was so happy about that... and Moses so angry.

TOM: What a stupid reason, to take such a spirit from this world, one who gave so much...

ALOIS: One who is still giving. My people will never forget him. I will not let them. They say he was… our fren… our pata… our tisa…our holiman.

TOM: Our friend… our father… our tisa… our saint.

ALOIS: Your pidgin is improving. Did you have a good tisa? …Yes, Pata Paddy, he was our martyr, was he not?

TOM: I suppose he was. And for what?

ALOIS: For love.

TOM: How… foolish.

ALOIS: Pata Tom… When you love someone, it is never foolish.

TOM: Alois, I hope you don't think that… I am… that somehow it was me that…

ALOIS: You give yourself too much credit. It was Moses killed him.

TOM: Moses needs to be brought to justice. He should be hanged. It's murder.

ALOIS: Yes.

TOM: He's a murderer.

ALOIS: Yes. But the Huli people believe…

TOM: I don't care about the Huli. He's a muderder.

ALOIS: …there is one offense worse than murder.

TOM: Now what would that be? Stealing, I suppose.

ALOIS: Yes. Stealing a person's innocence, stealing a person's moral fiber. It is adultery. The rape of someone's spirit. The abuse of someone's soul. More evil than taking a life.

TOM: Is Moses… Is the payback… Is it still… Should I be… concerned?

ALOIS: I advise you to be careful. Are you still going to Madang, to teach in the seminary?

TOM: I can't. Until there is a replacement. It will take some time. And I will be here by myself. Alois, I must tell you. I am terrified.

ALOIS: Your Capuchin brothers were here for Pata Paddy's funeral. You should have discussed this with them. You should have explained. They would remove you.

TOM: I couldn't. It's far too… complicated… I must do God's will.

ALOIS: I wonder, do we worship the same God? I have to be going.

ALOIS turns to leave, again.

TOM: Please don't leave me here alone.

ALOIS: Alone? You are hardly alone. What would Pata Paddy do? That is the question you must answer.

TOM: Yes…

ALOIS: I need you to tell me…

TOM: …what would Paddy do…

ALOIS: …did you make love to Clare?

TOM: …No. No, I… I wanted to. But… She ran off. I called after her. She was angry. I…

ALOIS: That's all, no more… I don't blame you. I blame no one. Except myself. Pata Paddy was right. You see, I had great love for Clare. And I like to think…

TOM: She was… easy to love…

ALOIS: …that she had a love for me, however small. In her bilum, I found this poem I left for her. *Takes it from his pocket.* She had it with her. I was hoping she would see it. Why would she have it with her if she didn't have… affection for me…?

TOM: A poem? Let me see.

ALOIS hands it to TOM, TOM glances at it.

TOM: My love has wings.

ALOIS: I put it there so she would find it. I don't know if... but she had it with her...

TOM: *Handing it back.* Yes, she showed it to me. Before she ran off.

ALOIS: She did? Why would she do that?

TOM: We were arguing. She was confused. Then... she just... ran off.

ALOIS: But why...

TOM: Why... yes, why...

ALOIS: That's the very reason I put it there, so she would know.

TOM: She knew.

ALOIS: She knew, then?

TOM: You see, I wanted... to make love to her. God forgive me. She showed me this... so I would know... she loved another. I understood... then she told me... it was you.

ALOIS: She said that? My Clare?

TOM: Yes.

ALOIS: She said she loved me? But why... would she then take her life?

TOM: Paddy thought she may have slipped and fallen.

ALOIS: No.

TOM: It's possible.

ALOIS: I don't think so.

TOM: Yes, she slipped and she fell.

ALOIS: Pata Tom, Clare could dance on one foot all night long, and never slip and fall. *Near tears.* Oh, how I loved to watch her dance... Oh, my Clare.

ALOIS begins to leave again.

TOM: Thank you, Alois.

ALOIS: *Hesitates, is short with him.* Thank me, for what?

TOM: For your forgiveness.

ALOIS: You thank me too soon.

TOM: I don't think so.

ALOIS: Pata Tom… I have a burning question… why did you become a priest?

TOM: You can't imagine what it means to be a priest in my family. My mother told everyone, since I was a boy. She was so proud. The celebration… went on for weeks. The power a priest has. The stature. Everyone looks up to a priest. There was never a question.

ALOIS: Never? Not even in your own heart?

TOM: Of course, we question things. We must. I thought… coming to the missions, it would wipe away all doubt…

ALOIS: Pata Paddy said, if we think only of ourselves, doubt is always our companion.

TOM: What do you… how could you… you have no idea how difficult it is, the suffering, the remorse, the agony of living with this, it is always there, always with you, so you work hard, you read, you teach, you go to the ends of the earth… and it follows you. See where it has brought me, oh god…

ALOIS: Lookim yu bihain, Pata Tom. Good-by.

Again, ALOIS tries to leave.

TOM: Alois, I'm…

ALOIS: Afraid?

TOM: Yes, the payback, you see… I…

ALOIS: I really must be going.

TOM: Please don't go.

ALOIS tries to leave, stops as TOM approaches him, desperate.

TOM: *Angry.* I forbid you to leave. You don't have my permission. Pata Paddy would not have you do this. Yes, think of that, how you would disappoint him. You must stay. *Changes his tone.* Alois, I can teach you so much. I'll give you my books. Yes, you love books. Paddy told me. You can have them all. This can all be yours. *Angry again.* Leave and you'll never have this chance again. Don't think you can come back anytime and expect the same... *Changes again.* ...Yes, yes you can, of course, you are welcome anytime. That's why you must stay. Precisely why you must not go. Such an opportunity for you, Alois. *Angry again.* You can't leave me here. You can't get even with people. It's sinful to retaliate. Is this your payback? You have to control your anger. You must stay. *A pause, then, pleading.* Alois, please...

ALOIS: *Smiles.* Pata Paddy, he gave us the answer. Of course.

TOM: *Cynically.* What could possibly be the answer?

ALOIS: He said, each day, huh? He always added that little smile, huh? Each day, he said, there is always... something new to forgive. Tru. Do you suppose... that is the reason to be a priest? Hmm?

ALOIS looks for some recognition of this thought from TOM, but does not get it.

ALOIS exits.

ALOIS'S comment adds to TOM'S burden.

SFX: Drums. Ominous.

TOM looks around the room, as if he has entered it for the first time, looking for a way out, and can't find it. The oppressive isolation descends on him as the stage goes to black.

END.

SUMISAMI

GLOSSARY

Title Page

Pata	[Fah -ta]
Alois	[Al' loys]

Act One

doti	*sloppy, dirty*
plis	*please*
kau kau	*sweet potato*
gaden	*garden*
waitim	*to wait for someone*
ol taim	*all the time*
olsem wanem	*How? Why? What's up with that?*
sicman	*patient, sick person*
belhat	*angry (no belhat — to not get angry)*
plis	*please*
tok	*talk*
pisin	*pidgin* (Pidgin English)
afta	*after*
Sande	*Sunday*
Fraide	*Friday*
raskols	*criminals*
laik	*like*
no wok	*doesn't work*
bagarap	*broken*
Inglis	*English*
yu bin skulim	*you've been*

SUMISAMI

mi	*teaching me*
me save	*my teacher* (sah-veh)
mi stop we	*near by, about*
klostu	*nearby*
fixim	*to fix*
planti	*plenty*
stilim	*to steal*
taim bepo	*history, time before*
raskols nogut	*damn rascals*
apinoon	*afternoon*
wagie	*name of river*
kam na kisim	*come and get it*
welcom yu	*you are welcome*
kumu	*greens, vegetables*
save man	*elder, wise man*
switmor	*sweet*
Tenkyu tru	*thank you very much*
welcom tru	*you're very welcome*
waitman	*whiteman*
kina shell	*precious shell, used as money*
gud	*good*
luk	*look*
ples masalai	*a sacred place*
riva	*river*
tink	*think*
nating	*nothing*
yu tink stori	*you think the story*

SUMISAMI

nating	*is nothing*
mangalim	*to want with great desire*
kamap	*come up*
bigpela	*high*
nam ba wan	*number one*
malum malum	*so very soft*
mangalim tru	*magic love*
sing sing	*tribal celebration with dancing, costumes, painted faces*
buai nut	*bee-tle nut, a nut natives mash and tobacco, for mild high*
rope i stop long leg	*rope tied onto leg*
tasel yu no kan lukim	*an invisible rope*
hepi	*happy*
yu laikim dispela stori	*you like this story*
moning	*morning*
gudpela	*good man*
lukim yu long now	*good-by, see you later*
bilum	*a woven cloth shoulder bag for carrying almost anything*
oli tok tok nating	*all the talk is nothing*
save	*understand* (sah-veh)

Act Two

Conversation between Alois and Moses.

    Huli, passim bilong yumi em olsem!
    Huli, this is how we do things

    Lotru wed okum ily-o!
    Real law is coming!

    Bulsit! Payback tru wed.
    Rubbish, payback is true law!

    Ekepu gvman okum ilyi-oi!
    New government is coming!

    Ekep ily mada inap, inap!
    Now that's enough, enough!

inap	*enough*
bandicoot	*small marsupial about the size of a rabbit*
tok gud Inglis	*talk good English*
tell yu tru	*I tell you the truth*

    Mi tink mi laikim Pata Tom.
    I think I like Fata Tom.

lista	*list*
lokup	*lock up*

    Pata Tom givim list long yu?
    Fata Tom give you a list?

    planti wok bilong yu mi tupela
    there is plenty of work for you and me

    man no gut   *a bad man*

trabelman	*a bad man*
skulim mi	*teaches me*
tisim	*teaches*
switheart	*boyfriend*
helpim	*help*
long long	*crazy*
olpela man	*old man*

Act Three

The end of the Our Father.

> Pogivim rong…bilong mipela
> *And forgive us our trespasses*

> Olsem mipela I pogivim ol arapela I mekim rong long mipela
> *As we forgive those who trespass against us*

> No rausim olgeta samting nogut long mipela. Amen.
> *And lead us not into temptation, but deliver us from evil. Amen.*

no haraip	*don't hurry, don't go so fast*
isi isi	*easy, go easy*
bilas	*costume*
bilong yu	*your, yours*
wapi	*war paint*
bilas long pes bilong mi	*my war paint*
papa bilongmi	*my father, our father*
yu kilim strong	*to thrash or kill a person*

no stretpela man   *not a good man*
yu no save tok tru   *you are not honest*
mitupela Huli   *we are Huli*
brata   *brothers*

The sign of the cross.
> Long nem bilong papa, na bilong young pela boy, na bilong Holi Spirit.
> *In the name of the father, the son and the Holy Spirit.*

respektim   *respect*
hepiman   *happy man*
gutnius   *bible*
mirikel   *miracle*

> olsem nau em bikpela samting kamap long yumi
> *and now you are doing something*
> na yumi ken amamas tru
> *about which we are proud*

fren   *friend*
pata   *father, priest*
tisa   *teacher*
holiman   *saint*
lookim yu bihain   *good-by*

About the Playwright

RAY WERNER is a Pittsburgh playwright and a member of the Dramatists Guild of America. In 2009 his *Night Song* was selected for The Source Festival in Washington D.C. In 2010 his trilogy *Elder Hostages*, after a staged reading at both The Community Theater in Cape Town SA and the Hazlett in Pittsburgh PA, premiered at The Pittsburgh Playwrights Theater in 2010, Mark Clayton Southers, Founding Artistic Director. Ray has had four one-acts in their Black and White Festival, including *Redneck Revenge* which was awarded the Audience Favorite. In 2018, The Pittsburgh Playwrights Theater premiered five new plays in the Ray Werner Play Festival, including *The Stuttering Pig, Christmas Tassel Bell, Raphael's Angels, Our Lady of Drubbleduffy,* and *SumiSami*. In 2019, PICT Irish and Classic Theater premiered the full length drama *Run the Rabbit Path* at the Fred Rogers Theater at WQED Pittsburgh.

The playwright is grateful

To the Capuchin Franciscans, St. Augustine Province, Pittsburgh PA.

To Fr. John Pfannenstiel and the Seraphic Mass Association for their help, their treasury of photographs, and the loan of their Capuchin habits and vestments.

To Bishop Bill Fey and Brother Ray Ronan for their extraordinary attention to the details of Papua New Guinea culture, and especially the spelling and diction of Tok Pisin. For your time, your enthusiasm and your blessing.

To Fr. Sam Driscoll for your encouragement when *SumiSami* was little more than a struggling idea.

A special thanks to director John Amplas for his talent, energy, and insight to bring *SumiSami* to the stage.

Pittsburgh Playwrights Theater is grateful for the support provided by The Pittsburgh Foundation, The Heinz Endowments Small Arts Initiative, Regional Asset District, Greater Pittsburgh Arts Council, The Pittsburgh Cultural Trust, Richard King Mellon Foundation, August Wilson Center-African American Cultural Center, The Opportunity Fund, and Advancing Black Arts in Pittsburgh Fund.

Proceeds from the sale of this book will go to help the Capuchins in Papua New Guinea.

Yupela i go long olgeta hap bilong graun na
telimautim gutnius long olgeta man
MAK 16:15

CPSIA information can be obtained
at www.ICGtesting.com
Printed in the USA
BVHW090512270621
610333BV00007B/15